Critical Acclaim for
Meaningful Differences
in the Everyday Experience of
Young American Children

"For those of us who have always suspected, **The Bell Curve** and similar arguments notwithstanding, that a child's early environment sets the stage for the rest of that child's life, this book represents a timely breakthrough. The data that Hart and Risley have accumulated are unique in the social sciences. And the story they tell is truly compelling. We've known for some time that a child's early environment was important, but Hart and Risley's data move us beyond this general observation. Their analysis of qualities of parenting that make the difference in a child's acquisition of language moves us from the general to the specific. Further, their data clearly reveal to us both the incredible advantage that parenting can bestow on a young child, and the devastating handicap it can create in its less optimal forms. Hart and Risley's data present a counterpunch to those who would have us believe that a child's destiny is mostly in his or her genes."

—Steven F. Warren, Ph.D.
Professor of Special Education and Psychology
Peabody College, Vanderbilt University

"Lucky the children whose parents read **Meaningful Differences** and take the findings to heart. The five features of parenting very young children that the authors find lead to increases in intellectual performance and can be learned and practiced. The result will not be 'just' more academically successful children, but children who are more fun to be with and parents who take greater delight in their role."

—Laura Walther Nathanson, M.D.
*author of **The Portable Pediatrician for Parents** and **Kidshapes:***
Helping Children Control Their Weight;
*Contributing Editor, **Parents** magazine*

"Hart and Risley build upon—but avoid the failures of—the 'War on Poverty' of the 60's, in seeking to prevent children *of* poverty from maturing into adults *in* poverty. Based on data derived from meticulously designed observational methodology, the authors offer findings arguing persuasively on behalf of an intervention strategy preparing children of welfare parents to acquire the cognitive tools necessary for achieving the 'American dream.' This strategy is rooted in a five-pronged parent–child language experience for children up to age three.

Students, practitioners, scholars, parents, and policymakers will savor this trailblazing demonstration of the efficacy of early language learning for helping children to achieve levels of intellectual performance requisite for success in later life."

—**Robert Perloff, Ph.D.**
Distinguished Service Professor Emeritus of Business Administration
and of Psychology, Joseph M. Katz Graduate School of Business
University of Pittsburgh

"An absorbing journey through the process of researching children's early language development and its implications for the future. Human, informative, and enlightening, it is a useful addition to our understanding of the first few years of life."

—**Geraldine Youcha**
*author of **Minding the Children:***
Child Care in America from Colonial Times to the Present

"In a time when the political climate does not support early intervention, Hart and Risley offer distinctive evidence suggesting that the early linguistic environments of young children have long-term effects on their language development and their school performance. This careful study provides a substantive analysis of the importance of parent talk to the developing child. Their findings span time, social classes, and ethnicity— suggesting that the early influences of parent–child interaction at home are a pervasive factor in children's development."

—**Ann P. Kaiser, Ph.D.**
Professor, Department of Special Education & Psychology
and Human Development, Peabody College, Vanderbilt University

"A uniquely powerful book that brings the reader into the homes and lives and word-learning experiences of 42 children, whose families are alike and different in interesting ways. This is scientific endeavor made real. The book is a must-read for those interested in children, families, early intervention, and social policy."

—**Mabel L. Rice, Ph.D.**
University Distinguished Professor, The University of Kansas

"Meaningful Differences in the Everyday Experience of Young American Children represents the final results of a remarkable research journey in which the authors undertake to answer some of the most basic questions about why early intervention in the lives of young disadvantaged children is neither early enough nor intervention enough. Instead of leaving it at that, however, the authors then provide a compelling discussion of the policy implications of their findings, pointing to the undeniable need for parent education as the only way to break the cycle of intergenerational transmission which they so richly describe."

—**Patton O. Tabors, Ed.D.**
Research Associate, Home-School Study of Language and Literacy Development, Graduate School of Education, Harvard University

"Most research on intelligence has centred on genetic causes, and has neglected the detailed investigation of possible environmental intermediaries. This very thorough study is a welcome exception; it documents the very unequal way toddlers learn language from their parents, depending on social class and parental intelligence, and deserves very careful study. The book is a model of how environmental factors in intelligence formation should be studied."

—**H. J. Eysenck, Ph.D., D.Sc.**
*Professor Emeritus of Psychology
University of London*

"This is an outstanding book, and of the greatest social policy relevance in the current period when all social class and racial differences are being misinterpreted as due to genetic differences.

In 1970, Peter Frey and I called for a cessation of studies on such differences in intelligence and achievement tests until there could be measured for each child an EIPQ Coefficient, that is, his or her "Environmental Intelligence Producing Quotient." Hart and Risley have provided such a study, in much greater subtlety and detail than we envisaged.

Current policy decisions on compensatory education, Head Start, and the like should take a moratorium until all policymakers have read this important book."

—**Donald T. Campbell, Ph.D.**
Professor Emeritus, University Professor of Sociology-Anthropology, Psychology, and Education, Lehigh University

Meaningful Differences

in the Everyday Experience of
Young American Children

❖ ❖ ❖ ❖

Meaningful Differences

in the Everyday Experience of Young American Children

❖ ❖ ❖ ❖

by

Betty Hart and Todd R. Risley
The University of Kansas

·P·A·U·L·H·
BROOKES
PUBLISHING C⁰   Baltimore • London • Toronto • Sydney

Paul H. Brookes Publishing Co.
Post Office Box 10624
Baltimore, Maryland 21285-0624

Typeset by Brushwood Graphics, Inc., Baltimore, Maryland.
Manufactured in the United States of America by
The Maple Press Company, York, Pennsylvania.

Library of Congress Cataloging-in-Publication Data
Hart, Betty, 1927–
    Meaningful differences in the everyday experience of young
American children / by Betty Hart and Todd R. Risley.
        p.   cm.
    Includes bibliographical references and index.
    ISBN 1-55766-197-9
    1. Children—Language—Social aspects—United
States—Longitudinal studies.   2. Poor—United States—Social
conditions—Longitudinal studies.   3. Language acquisition—
Parent participation—United States—Longitudinal studies.
4. Sociolinguistics— United States—Longitudinal studies.
5. Child development—United States—Longitudinal studies.
I. Risley, Todd, R.   II. Title.
LB1139.L3H279   1995
401'.93—dc20   95-3939
                                                                      CIP

British Library Cataloguing-in-Publication data are available from
the British Library.

This book is dedicated with fondness and admiration to the parents and their children.

Contents

Foreword
◆ ◆ ◆ ◆

Children acquire language for expression and interpretation—to share with other people what their beliefs, their desires, and their feelings are about. Anyone who cares about children, therefore, has every reason to care about how they learn language. This book is about the circumstances of early language learning and is built around one central aspect of that learning: the words of the language. Virtually all children begin to acquire a vocabulary of words in the second year of life, usually soon after the first birthday. This means that a child's home and family provide the circumstances for the emergence of language and word learning. The book begins with the basic facts about the vocabularies of 42 children from the time they first began to say words at about 1 year until they were about 3 years old, and it then goes on to describe the interactions with other persons in their families that formed the contexts for their word learning.

The study is contextualized in the history of the War on Poverty and the authors' own intervention efforts in that war with low-income children in the 1960s. They meticulously document the rationale for the study in this book by recounting the several studies and intervention programs that preceded it. The description of their earlier efforts and the ensuing frustrations that accompanied the "failed" outcomes is an object lesson in how programmatic research should be developed and where the research ideas ought to come from. And at the end, they come back to their earlier findings and frustrations with new insights from this study with which to reconsider the earlier data. The whole thing reads like a detective story of the most serious academic kind.

We have long known that children differ greatly in when they begin to learn language and how fast they learn once they begin. The children in this study did indeed differ. Some began to learn words with a learning trajectory that took off like a small rocket. But other children, who may even have begun to say words at about the same age, were much slower to get off the ground, and their trajectories were forever in the shadow of the other children. Why? That is the central question in this book.

In answering the question, Hart and Risley discovered that some things don't matter. For example, race/ethnicity doesn't matter; gender doesn't matter; whether a child is the first in the family or born later also doesn't matter. But what does matter, and it matters very much, is relative economic advantage. First, and this major theme sounds again and again in these pages to provide a baseline for what follows, children living in poverty, children born into middle-class homes, and children with professional parents *all have the same kinds of everyday language experiences*. They all hear talk about persons and things, about relationships, actions, and feelings, and about past and future events. And they all participate in interactions with others in which what they do is prompted, responded to, prohibited, or affirmed. But children in more economically privileged families hear some of these things more often, and others less often, than children in poverty and working-class homes. The differences between the families documented in this book were not in the kinds of experiences they provided their children but in the differing amounts of those experiences. The basic finding is that children who learn fewer words also have fewer experiences with words in interactions with other persons, and they are also children growing up in less economically advantaged homes.

Why do children differ so drastically in the trajectories of their word learning? It turns out that *frequency matters*. The powerful lesson to be learned in these pages is that even though they have the *same kinds* of experiences with language and interactions in their homes, children born into homes with fewer economic resources have fewer of these experiences. And the consequence is that they learn fewer words and acquire a vocabulary of words more slowly.

On the one hand, the importance of the frequency of experiences might not come as a surprise to many people; most theories of learning assume it. On the other hand, some very influential theories of language acquisition are built on the assumption that children need only hear something once in order to acquire it. A child might very well learn a word or some other aspect of language after hearing it only a single time. But the lesson in this book is clear: The more a child hears of one or another aspect of the language, the greater the opportunity the child has to learn it. Opportunities for learning are enhanced when children engage in many and varied interactions with other people, and individual families tend to be consistent in the opportunities they provide their children for such interactions over the crucial early years of language learning. As a result, some children learn more words than others, with a trajectory of word learning that takes off and flies, simply because they engage in many more interactions with language in their homes.

We certainly have known for a long time that children reared in poverty have far fewer opportunities for experiences of many kinds, language being just one of them. Other studies have pointed to one or another reason why that might be so. Parenting is a challenge in the best of circumstances, and being relatively undereducated and poor makes it that much harder. As parents are faced with the challenges and frustrations, many things have to give, social interactions and talk among them. Children in families with low incomes surely have still other quality experiences that are different from those quantified here—experiences that are culturally valid and contribute in positive ways to their development. But they are evidently not having the experiences with language that enhance word learning in the early years.

The easy reaction to these findings would be "we already know" that children living in the lowest economic circumstances in this country do not have the same language experiences other children have. But I, for one, know of no one else who has done what Hart and Risley have done. They went into the homes of 42 children, month after month, during the most crucial 2-year period in a child's language learning career. And carefully, conscientiously, sensitively, and thoroughly, they found out why the trajectories of word learning can differ so dramatically among different children.

Collecting data is relatively easy; anyone can follow a child around with a tape recorder or ask a parent to record a child's words in a diary or checklist of words. But collecting and processing a database of this quality from 42 families required a heroic effort. The main result concerning vocabulary acquisition may well be what many would have expected. However, the longitudinal data showing what was happening in these homes during the time of early vocabulary growth are a major contribution. And the finding is heartbreaking that by the time the children were 3 years old, *parents* in less economically favored circumstances had said fewer different words in their cumulative monthly vocabularies than had the *children* in the most economically advantaged families in the same period of time.

The authors do not stop there. They conclude by outlining an agenda for intervention that begins in the home and begins very early in a young child's life, with a focus on the social influences on language and its acquisition within the cultural context of the family. This book is making its appearance now, decades after the War on Poverty was joined, in a political climate filled with tension between genuine concern for poor children and strong dissatisfaction with our welfare system. But the clear message here is that the welfare of poor children can only be served by enhancing the experiences they receive at home—by making the vocabulary and language they will need for expression and interpretation, in the wider contexts of their lives, available to them from those who care for them and also care about them. I hope this book will find its way into the hands of everyone with an interest in children and concern for their present and future lives.

Lois Bloom, Ph.D.
Teachers College
Columbia University
New York

Preface
◆◆◆◆

*T*his book is the first of several planned to report findings from a longitudinal database unique both in its size and in the richness of the picture it provides of the everyday lives of American families. For more than 2 years we observed 1- and 2-year-old children growing up in the kinds of families everyone knows but does not talk about very much: the "ordinary" families who are coping, who are fairly happy, and whose children are reasonably well-behaved and working at grade level in school.

We have written this book primarily for a community of ordinary informed readers. We have placed the research data within the text in "pictures" that can be skimmed, because we hope no specialized knowledge or advanced education is required to understand our research, why and how we worked as we did, and what we found out about what parents do during their everyday interactions with their children that has lasting influence on their children's development.

We have also included the research data in much greater detail in tables and appendices to invite the thorough appraisal of our professional colleagues who are natural scientists and so are trained to look beyond common perceptions of the world and critically and carefully test perceptions of what is true and of how each truth relates to other truths in lawful ways.

In this first book, we report on the families and on what the children received from their experience with their parents. In a second book, we plan to report on how the children developed and on what they did with what they received from their parents. We report first on the families because we undertook the longitudinal study to find out what was happening to children at home when they were just beginning to talk.

Our research began during the 1960s, when there was a surge of public faith in the power of the environment and widespread hope that pressing social problems could be solved by improving the everyday experiences of American children. In the 1980s, when we were collecting and analyzing the data from the longitudinal research, we saw the failure of that hope producing a reluctant acceptance that if people were unchangeable, then so were their prospects. The current surge in attention to the role of heredity in human accomplishments contributes to an unfortunate political presumption that the minimally competent might have to be written off and the working class left to sort themselves out, as they have done traditionally, in terms of upward mobility.

In fact, despite shifts in public and professional attention, the fundamental consensus among scientists has not changed: Experience and heredity contribute about equally to human functioning. Of course in the human species, genetics contributes both to the general competence of parents and children and to specific social behaviors of parenting and childing that influence the experience children receive. But beyond the contribution of genetics, all societies assume that experience can be enhanced and supplemented to improve the competencies of children and that those competencies will become part of the inheritance they pass on to their children. Our research happens to focus on the contribution of early experience and on which parts of that experience are important.

The difficulty in the 1960s was that people placed their hope in the power of phenomena that science had hardly begun to understand. Now that we know a little more about what children's early experience is like, we have written this book to tell you about it.

About the Authors
❖❖❖❖

Betty Hart, Ph.D., and Todd R. Risley, Ph.D., began their careers in the early 1960s at the Institute for Child Development at the University of Washington, where they participated in the original demonstrations of the power of learning principles in influencing young children. With Montrose Wolf they introduced the basic procedures of *adult attention* and *time-out* now routinely taught and used in teaching and parenting. They also introduced the procedures for *shaping speech and language* widely used in special education.

In 1965, Hart and Risley began 30 years of collaborative work at The University of Kansas, when they established preschool intervention programs in poverty neighborhoods in Kansas City. Their study of what children actually do and say in day care and preschool and their publications on *incidental teaching* form the empirical base for contemporary child-centered teaching practices in preschool and special education.

Dr. Hart is now Professor Emeritus of Human Development at The University of Kansas, and Dr. Risley is Professor of Psychology at the University of Alaska. Both are Senior Scientists at the Schiefelbusch Institute for Life Span Studies at The University of Kansas.

Dr. Risley's other work has been on abnormal development and behavioral treatments. He has served on many national boards and commissions, as Editor of the *Journal of Applied Behavior Analysis*, as President of the Association for Advancement of Behavior Therapy and of the behavioral division of the American Psychological

Association, and as Alaska's Director of Mental Health and Developmental Disabilities. Dr. Hart has remained focused on the language development of preschool children.

Acknowledgments
◆ ◆ ◆ ◆

*T*he immense database of longitudinal observations could not exist without the help of many, many people, and one of our rewards is an opportunity to thank most of them by name.

We have dedicated this book to those whom research consent forms stipulate we cannot name: the parents and their children who are its real authors. They can never be thanked enough for sharing their personal warmth, their individual complexity, and the diversity of their daily lives. From the copy of the book we are sending each of them, we hope that each of them will know how deep and lasting have been our respect and affection. We are as grateful for our matchless memories of everyday parenting as we are for the objective data that permit us to examine influences on children.

We are grateful for the 10 years of support by Grant HD03144 from the National Institute of Child Health and Human Development to the Bureau of Child Research (now the Schiefelbusch Institute for Life Span Studies) and the Department of Human Development at The University of Kansas. We especially thank those people who so generously and selflessly provided their wisdom and the supportive context that enabled us to stay focused on the research: Sid Bijou, Dick Schiefelbusch, Fran Horowitz, Jim Sherman, Vance Hall, Charlie Greenwood, and Steve Schroeder. We also acknowledge with gratitude the unfailing help of the administrative staff at the university, especially Paul Diedrich and Ed Zamarippa, and the staff at the Juniper Gardens Children's Project, especially Mary Williard and Betty Smith.

We remain in awe of the masterful creation of Rebecca Finney, the computer programmer who designed the data entry, coding, data analysis, and reliability assessments for the database, ever attentive to circumventing human error and putting structures in place that we had yet to realize we needed in order to answer our research questions.

We are deeply beholden to those whose daily dedication made possible the research reported here: to Maxine Preuitt and Liz Haywood, who conscientiously collected and painstakingly coded the data; and to Sheila Hoffman and Shirley Young, who persisted without complaint in the seemingly interminable task of accurately entering the data into computer files. We owe a lasting debt to them and to the many others who helped with the data, most notably Jennifer Lattimore.

It is gratifying to express our appreciation to Janet Marquis, David Thissen, and Peter Bentler for their gifts of statistical expertise; to John Wright, John Reiser, and Steve Warren for guiding our thinking about analyzing and reporting the data; to Fowler Jones for his patience and objectivity in testing the children; and to Dale Walker for sharing her data and her personal experiences with the children when they were in third grade.

Very special thanks are due to Maxine Preuitt, who put up with us for more than 25 years and shared her knowledge and insights into what it was like to grow up in poverty in Juniper Gardens.

Equally special thanks are owed to our benefactor Dick Schiefelbusch, who graciously enabled us to participate in his vision of a better world.

But our deepest gratitude and admiration must be reserved for our mentor, the great Montrose Wolf, who taught us to look directly at the world in order to learn how it really works and to concern ourselves with trying to solve the real problems of real people.

Years of work collecting and analyzing data are not really done until the results are publicly shared, and that requires help from many more people. Our colleagues had told us that the people at Brookes Publishing had the reputation of combining exceptional professionalism with generous consideration for what authors were trying to say. So we were not surprised, just pleased and thankful for the marvelous care everyone at Brookes took of us and the book. We are also grateful to Steve Warren and a number of anonymous reviewers for their discerning comments on the manuscript. A special debt of gratitude is owed to Lois Bloom for the perceptive and thoughtful rigor with which she addressed both the details of the research and the issues of the book.

Meaningful Differences

in the Everyday Experience of
Young American Children

CHAPTER ONE

Intergenerational Transmission of Competence

❖ ❖ ❖ ❖

*A*merica in the 1960s found a cause worth commit-
ting to: the War on Poverty. The aim was to in-
terrupt the cycle of poverty—the economic
disadvantages arising from employment disadvantages,
which had their sources in the educational disadvantages that resulted from growing up in poverty. An at-
tack was mounted on two fronts: breaking down barriers
to the advantages mainstream society enjoyed, and providing a boost up through job training and early education. Desegregation laws removed barriers to jobs,
housing, and educational institutions. Job training programs and early education programs provided a boost up
into the job market and the school system.

Because poverty was differentially prevalent among
minorities, racial discrimination had to be targeted. But
race, rather than the cycle of poverty, was a central issue
only in designing strategies to preserve cultural identity
within mainstream society. Early education programs
such as Head Start were funded to serve African American children in inner-city ghettos, Native American

children isolated on reservations, and white children in rural Appalachia. All across the country, experts in early childhood education designed intervention programs to give children isolated in poverty the social and cognitive experiences that underlay the academic success of advantaged children.[1] It was thought the War on Poverty could change children's lives within a generation.

Events continue to remind us that the War on Poverty did not succeed. After barriers were removed and a boost up was provided, the people who had the knowledge and skills that could influence and motivate the next generation of children moved away and left those less competent isolated in communities riddled with drugs, crime, unemployment, and despair. Like most wars, the War on Poverty was more successful in destroying the past than in creating the future, the competencies for participating in an increasingly technological society.

Competence as a social problem is still with us. American society still sees many of its children enter school ill-prepared to benefit from education. Too many children drop out of school and follow their parents into unemployment or onto welfare, where they raise their children in a culture of poverty. The boost up from early intervention during the War on Poverty did not solve the problem of giving children the competencies they need to succeed in school. We recognize now that by the time children are 4 years old, intervention programs come too late and can provide too little experience to make up for the past.

Early Intervention Programs

The intervention programs of the War on Poverty, the first efforts, were modeled on the booster shot. It was assumed that a concentrated dose of mainstream culture would be enough to raise intellectual performance and lead to success in mainstream schools. Children disadvantaged from living in isolated areas were brought into preschool programs similar to those advantaged children attended. The programs offered the enriched materials and activities available in such preschools, but replaced the traditional emphasis on social development with an emphasis on compensatory education, especially language and cognitive development.

Innovative curricula were designed and field tested. The content and objectives of the curricula were selected to teach in the preschool the competencies advantaged children apparently acquired at home. All of these curricula programmed successive educational experiences using materials especially designed to help children master basic academic skills in the style originated by Montessori for teaching poor children in Italy. DARCEE of Gray and Klaus, Karnes's GOAL, DISTAR of Bereiter and Englemann, and others are examples of the language and cognitive development curricula that were designed during the War on Poverty.[2]

Programs differed in emphasis and teaching methods, depending on theoretical orientation. Psychodynamic theory led to an emphasis on motivation and self-concept in the Bank Street program. In the Perry Preschool Project, the program, derived mainly from Piagetian theory, emphasized learning through activities and experiences to stimulate children to construct concepts and develop logical modes of thought. The behavioral orientation of the Bereiter-Englemann program emphasized highly structured direct instruction, including pattern drill.

Major improvements in language and cognitive performance were often immediate and large and were not

3

unique to any particular curriculum or theoretical approach. The improvements in performance were apparent in the preschool and carried over into the home. Although parents did not necessarily appreciate the changes in their children's behavior, they accepted the increases in activity and curiosity that resulted from the enriched experiences. Lateral and horizontal diffusion of the curricula content spread the effects beyond the child into the family and community. Head Start is still in existence because long-term benefits did accrue from early intervention programs; the children did adapt better to school and many stayed through school into adulthood with their age-mates.

But the academic headstart was temporary. In kindergarten, children who had not attended preschool programs caught up with the children who had. By the third grade the effects of the boost had washed out, and there was little difference in academic performance between children who had and had not taken part in early intervention programs. Scholastic achievement scores were similar to those before the War on Poverty. By the 1970s, intervention experts were wondering how they could possibly have believed that a single shot of mainstream culture would be sufficient to make substantial changes in intellectual performance in all or most children raised in poverty.

Intervention at the Turner House Preschool

Early in the War on Poverty, civic leaders in an African American community, the impoverished Juniper Gardens area of Kansas City, Kansas, joined representatives of the Bureau of Child Research at The University of Kansas in Lawrence to develop a community-based program of research designed to improve the educational and developmental experiences of the neighborhood children. They persuaded the Episcopal Diocese of Kansas to tear down a church in Juniper Gardens and build a community center, Turner House, and then called in a cadre of applied psychologists expert in remediating and generalizing behavior. We (the authors) brought our experience with clinical language intervention to design a half-day program for the Turner House Preschool. Instead of focusing on a theory-based curriculum designed to affect a hypothetical construct we could measure or estimate only from tests, we designed an intervention focused on the everyday language the children were using.

We focused on children's spontaneous speech as the best dynamic measure of cognitive functioning and as the behavior most likely to influence the educational value of people's responses.[3] Rather than evaluate the results of an intervention program by how children performed on IQ tests administered outside the intervention setting, we looked for improvements in how the children functioned in their daily activities in the preschool. We wanted the children to know more, but we also wanted to see them applying that knowledge, using language to elicit information and learning opportunities from their teachers in the preschool. We watched what the children were doing to guide what we were doing.

We developed reliable recording methods so that we could sample each child's spontaneous speech during preschool free play every day, recording all the utterances the child produced during a 15-minute observation. When data from a particular child were processed by computer, for each observation a list was derived of each different word encountered in the data; that list was compared to the master list of all the different words so far recorded for that child, and any word not already on the list was added. In this way an individual dictionary was compiled for each child that contained all the different words the child produced during the observation. We used this dictionary as a measure of the child's vocabulary.

Vocabulary Growth

A vocabulary is the stock of words (or signs) available to a person or a language community. The vocabulary comprises all the words a person "knows," both those a person can understand and those a person can use appropriately. New experiences add new words to the vocabulary and refine or elaborate the meanings of known words. Unlike other aspects of language, vocabulary continues to grow throughout life, increasing with each gain in experience and understanding. Because the vocabulary that individuals can command reflects so well their intellectual resources, we still have oral examinations, and vocabulary plays a major role in tests of intelligence.

We used vocabulary growth rather than IQ test scores as our measure of accumulated experience. This had several advantages. This measure was culturally unbiased: any word could increment total vocabulary resources, rather than solely words from a circumscribed set standard in mainstream culture. We could obtain repeated measures without the child memorizing a test, and we could infer from the child's use of a word in context what the child took to be the meaning of the word. The records of the words said in spontaneous speech during the varied activities and contexts of preschool free play gave us repeated samples of each child's vocabulary resources.

From the repeated samples of a child's vocabulary resources we could draw a developmental trajectory of vocabulary growth.[4] After we had recorded enough samples so that all the high-frequency words (articles, pronouns, verbs such as "get" and "go," nouns such as "mom" and "teacher") were listed in a child's individual dictionary, we could look at growth, the developmental trajectory formed by adding words to the dictionary, as a child either drew words from known vocabulary into daily use or learned new words from experiences such as those presented in intervention. The data from successive observations were displayed for each child as a developmental trajectory, or a cumulative vocabulary growth curve.

Intervention on Spontaneous Speech

Our interventions focused on designing effective teaching strategies. Rather than design a curriculum, we replicated the laboratory model of the University of Washington where we had been trained; we used its curriculum content and objectives to teach children the necessary preacademic competencies. We concentrated our efforts on developing strategies that would encourage children to display and elaborate in their everyday language what they learned from the planned experiences of the curriculum. We used our spontaneous speech samples to measure improvements and evaluate the effectiveness of the teaching procedures.

We designed strategies to teach children to imitate complex sentence constructions and to attend to topic words in others' speech.[5] We designed the procedures for directed discussion to teach children to notice and comment on more and more varied features of stories and pictures. We designed the procedures for narration training to help children sequence and relate the features they described. To encourage the children to display and extend what they learned from small-group sessions into the everyday play activities of the preschool, we designed incidental teaching. Incidental teaching focused teachers' attention during free play on active listening preparatory to selecting responses that would both appreciate what a child said and show enthusiastic interest in hearing still more. Every time a child initiated talk to a teacher, the teacher confirmed the child's topic and asked the child to elaborate; if necessary, the teacher modeled an elaboration, asked the child to imitate, and then confirmed the child's response.

As we developed effective teaching procedures and reliable methods for recording and analyzing children's spontaneous speech, we found ourselves confronting more and more often the assumption underlying intervention. Undertaking to remediate, improve, or add to present skill levels assumes the existence of some "difference," "delay," or "deficit" relative to a norm. But when we listened to the Turner House Preschool children talk during free play, they seemed fully competent to us, well able to explain and elaborate the topics typical in preschool interactions. We became increasingly uncertain about which language skills we should be undertaking to improve. We decided we needed to know, not from our textbooks, but from advantaged children, what skilled spontaneous speech at age 4 is in terms of grammar and content. We felt naively confident that if we knew what the skills were, we could teach them to the Turner House children.

Comparing Language Use

The Laboratory Preschool at The University of Kansas provided us a setting and program very similar to that at the Turner House Preschool. The children at the Laboratory Preschool, though, were primarily professors' children; from these advantaged children we might learn the upper boundaries of skill in spontaneous speech at age 4. We began to record in each setting, each week over a preschool year, identical samples of the children's spontaneous speech during preschool free play. Although at the time (1968) all the children at the Turner House Preschool were African American, and all the children at the Laboratory Preschool were white, we referred to them as children from families in poverty and professors' children to remind ourselves of the critical difference between them: the advantages available to professors' families, regardless of race, and the disadvantages experienced by families caught in the cycle of poverty.

We learned from the computer processing of the data that in similar activity settings the children in the two preschools talked about much the same things in much the same ways. Although the specific words were sometimes different, the functions of language were the same. In both settings the children asked questions, made demands, and described what they were doing. The difference was in how much talking went on. Most of the professors' children talked at least twice as much as the Turner House children. They talked about more different aspects of what they were doing; they asked more questions about how things worked and why.

We intervened with incidental teaching at the Turner House Preschool and easily increased the amount of talking that went on among the children during preschool free play. All the children began to talk more, both to teachers and among themselves. The spontaneous speech samples showed that when the Turner House children talked as much as the professors' children, they also asked as many questions and used as many different words as those children did.[6]

We had expected the vocabulary resources of the professors' children to be greater than those of children from families in poverty, and our estimates from the spontaneous speech samples showed just that. What surprised us, though, was the richness of the vocabulary in the everyday speech of the professors' children. We were so used to the appropriateness of what the Turner House children said during free play that we did not realize how extensive were the topics and how varied were the comments 4-year-olds could display in casual conversation. The difference in the extent of the vocabulary resources the Turner House children were drawing on became even more apparent after the children began to talk as much as the professors' children and to use as many different words during free play. The professors' children simply seemed to know more about everything.

Comparing Vocabulary Growth

We were less concerned with the smaller vocabularies, though, than with the flatter growth curves we saw. For the Turner House children, the rate of adding words to the dictionary in daily use was markedly slower than the rate at which the professors' children were adding words as is shown in Figure 1. We saw slower growth in the past, resulting in a smaller vocabulary at age 4, and slower growth continuing in the children's present interactions with experience. Projecting the developmental

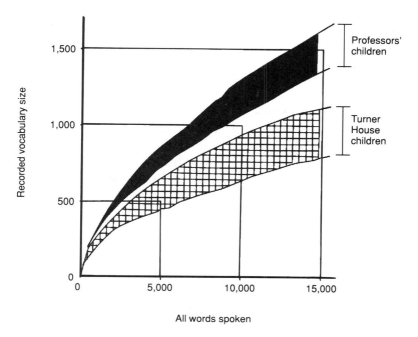

Figure 1.   The widening gap found between the vocabulary growth curves of the professors' children and the Turner House Preschool children. (See Appendix B for a detailed explanation of this figure.) (Adapted from Hart & Risley, 1981.)

trajectories of the growth curves into the future, we could see an ever-widening gap between the vocabulary resources the Turner House children and the professors' children would bring to school. This seemed to predict the reality of the findings of school research: that in high school many children from families in poverty lack the vocabulary used in more advanced textbooks.[7]

The vocabulary growth rates were strongly associated with rates of cognitive growth: The differences in the size of the children's recorded vocabularies in the two preschool groups were of the same magnitude as the differences in the children's scores on the Peabody Picture Vocabulary Test.[8] Clearly, the children enrolled in the Turner House Preschool were learning more slowly than the professors' children; what we knew of their families suggested that the children were not dissimilar from their parents and siblings. We could not reject heredity as an explanation for the differences we saw. But neither could we yield without asking whether the gap in rates of vocabulary growth was related to the immense gulf in the amount and richness of daily experience we saw separating the advantaged children of professors and the children from families in poverty.

Intervention on Vocabulary Growth Rate

We knew what the goal of our intervention needed to be: changing the developmental trajectory. We needed to accelerate the rate at which the Turner House children added words to their dictionaries in daily use. We considered possible sources of the differences we saw in vocabulary growth rates and proposed three hypotheses for investigation. The first hypothesis concerned cultural differences, the second experience, and the third mediated experience. We randomly assigned the Turner House children to experimental and control groups to test each hypothesis in turn.[9]

The first hypothesis proposed that the vocabulary growth curves drawn from the spontaneous speech data were not measuring the true extent of the children's vocabulary resources, because a preschool setting designed for advantaged white children did not call upon African American children from families in poverty to use the vocabulary resources they actually had in their interactions with materials and people. One of our African American teachers was immersed in studying her culture; she arranged for the experimental-group children a preschool setting that duplicated the living room in most of the children's homes. The room had a carpet, sofa, and television set; there were magazines, dolls, battery-operated toys, household utensils, clothing, and linens. As the children engaged in familiar activities with these materials, the teachers talked with them just as always. Over the 8 months of study, the vocabulary growth curves drawn from the spontaneous speech data recorded for the children in the home-like setting showed no acceleration relative to the curves of the control-group children in the traditional preschool setting. In both contexts the children were drawing equally on their vocabulary resources.

The second hypothesis proposed that the slower vocabulary growth of the Turner House children was due to a lack of the extensive and varied experiences available to advantaged children. We arranged for the experimental-group children a series of field trips to enrich the experiences they had to talk about during preschool free play. After 6 months of weekly field trips, we did not see any acceleration in vocabulary growth curves. But the experimental-group children did not talk about the field trip experiences after they returned to the preschool; they, like the control-group children, talked about what they were doing at the moment during free play.

The third hypothesis proposed that the slower vocabulary growth of the Turner House children was due not merely to a lack of the extensive and varied experiences of advantaged children, but to a lack of adult mediation. Teachers needed to mediate field trip experiences by directing children's attention, and describing and explaining, so that the children could relate each experience to what they already knew. For the next year we arranged a new series of field trip experiences in which all the children in the preschool participated. But only the experimental-group children had small-group discussions before and after each field trip.

Before the group went on a field trip to a bank, for example, the teacher and the experimental-group children talked about and handled money, discussed reasons for wanting to save money and what people bought with savings (cars, stereos, toys), the need for a secure place to put money, and how people put money into banks, kept track of it while it was there, and took it out again when they wanted to buy something. On the field trip the teachers deposited and withdrew money from a bank account, explaining each step to the watching children. After returning from the field trip, the teacher and the experimental-group children sat down to talk about what they had seen; they reviewed all the steps in depositing and withdrawing money, using vocabulary words such as "teller," "deposit slip," and "checking account." They talked about who worked in a bank and what jobs people did there as the teacher encouraged children to comment and ask questions.

Following each field trip the teachers set up a free-play area in the preschool with all the materials needed to role play the experience. The area gave children an opportunity to use the vocabulary they had been exposed to on the field trip and prompted talking about the experience during preschool free play when samples of their spontaneous speech were being recorded. For example, teachers set up a banking area where children could role play depositing and withdrawing play money using checkbooks, deposit slips, and savings books.

All the children eagerly engaged with all the new materials and activities introduced in the preschool. The spontaneous speech data showed a spurt of new vocabulary words added to the dictionaries of all the children and an abrupt acceleration in their cumulative vocabulary growth curves. But just as in other early intervention programs, the increases were temporary. The faster growth rates did not continue once the new vocabulary appropriate to the novel preschool materials had been drawn into use.

An End and a Beginning

We found we could easily increase the size of the children's vocabularies by teaching them new words. But we could not accelerate the rate of vocabulary growth so that it would continue beyond direct teaching; we could not change the developmental trajectory. However many new words we taught the children in the preschool, it was clear that a year later, when the children were in kindergarten, the effects of the boost in vocabulary resources would have washed out. The children's developmental trajectories of vocabulary growth would continue to point to vocabulary sizes in the future that were increasingly discrepant from those of the professors' children.

We learned the universal lesson of the War on Poverty: Removing barriers and offering opportunities and incentives is not enough to overcome the past, the transmission across generations of a culture of poverty. Like our contemporaries in this war, we had put our best efforts and all our accumulated knowledge into our interventions. We had been so sure that mediated experience would change how the children responded to the world.

15

But we saw that by the age of 4, when the children had become competent users of the syntax and pragmatic functions of their language, patterns of vocabulary growth were already established and intractable. We saw increasing disparity between the extremes—the fast vocabulary growth of the professors' children and the slow vocabulary growth of the Turner House children. Again we contemplated the power of heredity to explain the differences; again we decided against ceding the field before we fully understood the developmental trajectories we saw.

The Meaning of Vocabulary Growth Curves

The one clear success of our interventions was the choice to focus on vocabulary use as a dynamic measure of cognitive functioning. The differences in vocabulary size we saw at age 4 were undoubtedly influenced by inherited differences in cognitive capacity. But the *influence of differences in demands for cognitive functioning*, as evidenced in vocabulary use during children's everyday experiences at home, remained unknown. We had, however, the measure we needed in order to examine that unknown.

A vocabulary growth curve provides a direct and continuous measure of a child's intellectual functioning that does not require the hypothetical constructs and statistical assumptions of an IQ test. The growth of the vocabulary in use directly reflects the increasing complexity of the symbols a child learns to manipulate relative to everyday experience. We did not need to infer cognitive growth from monitoring a child's periodic performance on a small set of standardized test items: We could measure learning while it was happening.

But if we were to understand how and when differences in developmental trajectories began, we needed to see what was happening to children at home at the very beginning of their vocabulary growth. We needed to know what an average vocabulary growth rate is in order to ask whether children who learn vocabulary faster have parents who regularly provide those children something different or something more than the parents of children who have average vocabulary growth rates. We did not even know exactly what the parents of children with average vocabulary growth rates were doing on a daily basis that might influence the complexity of the symbols their children were manipulating. Before we surrendered to the power of heredity and accepted vocabulary growth as part of an instinctive response to exposure to language, we needed to find out whether or not parents actually *do* anything during their everyday interactions with their children that makes a lasting difference in how fast their children's vocabularies grow.

Endnotes

1. For a historical perspective, see the report from a symposium concerned with early intervention programs and the issues as seen in the 1960s (Brottman, 1968).
2. The work of Montessori (1912) is interesting because her goal was to provide basic educational experience to poor children viewed at the time not as "disadvantaged" but in need of the kinds of experiences other children routinely got at home.

   Among the preschool curricula designed were DARCEE (Gray & Klaus, 1968), GOAL (Karnes, Hodgins, Stoneburner, Studley, & Teska, 1968), and DISTAR (Bereiter & Englemann, 1966). Specified curricula, not formally named, were designed for the Milwaukee Project (Garber, 1988), the Bank Street program (Deutsch, 1967), and the Perry Preschool Project (Weikart, Bond, & McNeil, 1978). Weikart (1972) reported a planned comparison of three curricula; children learned equally well in all three as long as each was well and enthusiastically implemented by the teachers.

   A brief and especially perceptive discussion of the issues as perceived in 1971 is found in Stanley (1972).

   A report on how the children turned out, plus a review of the early programs, is the integrative study of Lazar and Darlington (1982).

   That the issues are still very much with us, and how they are perceived in 1991, may be seen in Huston (1991).
3. For an overview of our approach, see Risley, Hart, and Doke (1971); the observation system used during preschool free play is described in Hart (1983).
4. We described the rationale for and discussed the significance of the cumulative vocabulary growth curve as a developmental trajectory in Hart and Risley (1981).
5. Teaching procedures we developed and tested were Imitation training (Risley & Reynolds, 1970), Directed discus-

sion/Narration training (Risley, 1977b), and Incidental teaching (Hart & Risley, 1975, 1978, 1982).

6. The measures and outcomes from this comparison of professors' and Turner House children's language are reported in Hart and Risley (1980).

7. The results of years of intervention in public school classrooms was reported in Becker (1977); interventions brought children's academic performance up to grade level in all areas except vocabulary, and Becker recommended direct vocabulary instruction in later grades.

8. The Peabody Picture Vocabulary Test (Dunn, 1965) was administered to each child at the end of the preschool year.

9. This research is described more fully in Hart (1982).

CHAPTER TWO

Sampling Children's Developmental Experience

❖ ❖ ❖ ❖

*T*he vocabulary growth rates we saw in the preschool data seemed unalterable by intervention by the time the children were 4 years old. We saw all the children readily satisfying the social requirements to be clear, pertinent, and responsive; and we realized that everyday conversation does not require competent speakers to use an enriched vocabulary. Whatever environmental pressures prompted the use of enriched vocabulary, and so gave rise to differences in vocabulary growth rates, must have been at work before the children came to preschool. If we were to understand vocabulary growth, we needed data on what parents and children were so routinely doing together that it could add up to the differences we saw.

When we went to the literature, we realized we were going to have to get the data ourselves. Like other child development professionals, we knew how children grow and develop language.[1] But we did not know when and how children's language experience changes in amount and kind as new skills are learned and how often, for example, parents interact with the cuddly 1-year-old who has turned into a sassy or rebellious 2-year-old. We also knew the parenting literature,[2] but we did not know how often parents actually behave in the ways they report or how, for example, parents convey achievement demands or demands for enriched vocabulary to their children on a daily basis.

We knew the anthropological studies[3] describing how children grow up in different cultures and different homes. But we did not know, for example, what parents actually tell their children about how to talk and act like a member of a particular social group or how often such conversations take place. We also knew the considerable literature on how parents behave with their children in laboratory settings[4] when they have stimulating and age-appropriate materials and there are no siblings and no telephone or television to distract or compete with interaction. But we did not know how often parents interact in the same way at home or how often such optimal conditions occur during a typical day.

We had the additional benefit of personally knowing hundreds of children and their parents. Over the years in our infant, toddler, and preschool child care settings, we had heard innumerable descriptions of what goes on in children's homes. But from all our experience and reading about how parents interact with their children; about children's physical, social, cognitive, and language development; and about child-rearing practices in many cultures, we found we could not describe exactly how much and what kinds of experience children actually have within a family on a day-to-day basis.

Why are there so few longitudinal data about what goes on in children's homes?[5] We found out when we decided to collect these data ourselves. Doing a longitudinal study means keeping it going year after year. It means keeping the families even though they may be unreliable, keeping a schedule so that there are no gaps in the data, keeping the staff in whom training time and expense have been invested, and keeping the measurements accurate so there is no bias or drift in the data. All this has to be done, regularly and carefully, for many years before any results emerge. Such a study runs on the hope that the families and staff will not quit, on the faith that the child's cumulative experience is being accurately captured in the measures, and on the charity of funding sources.

The Best-Laid Plans

When we described to a senior colleague our intent to do a longitudinal study, she said, "You're crazy," and she was right. Before we were 2 months into the study, we were wondering whether we could call it all off. Although we knew that it takes at least 8 hours to transcribe 1 hour of audiotape, we had not fully realized the amount of work we were deliberately assigning ourselves for the next 6 years.

We started out with grand ambitions: We would recruit 120 families and observe each family for 1 hour each month for 1 year. Then we would select 60 of the families whose daily lives were most typical of socioeconomic and sociocultural groups and drop the rest. We had recruited only 10 families before we knew that observing 120 families for an hour each month would require more than twice the trained staff we had available. We had only one family drop out before we knew we did not want to spend time transcribing data we would never use. And we could foresee even then how difficult it would be to tell a family, "Thank you, we are done." When people are generous enough to allow observation in their homes, it is very hard to stop.

We thought we might be able to observe 120 families if we collected fewer data and went to each home every other month instead of each month. We decided instead that we would rather observe fewer families and know more about each of them. Also, rapport would be easier to build and maintain if we visited the family each month, and the family would be less likely to forget the schedule of observations. But chiefly, more frequent observations would give us a richer, more representative picture of a family, especially through the changes in circumstances as the child learned to talk. The more observations we had, the more likely we were to find out what was truly typical of family interactions. We could, for example, split the data into two sets, consisting of observations from every other month (even- and odd numbered months),[6] in order to verify the stability of what we saw going on in the family.

Our ambition was to record "everything" that went on in children's homes—everything that was done by the children, to them, and around them. Because we were committed to undertaking the labor involved in observing and transcribing, and because we did not know exactly which aspects of children's cumulative experience were contributing to establishing rates of vocabulary growth, the more information we could get each time we were in the home the more we could potentially learn. But we ruled out videotape as too expensive, cumbersome, and intrusive. As it turned out, we had quite enough problems with fouled audiotapes and malfunctioning tape recorders.

We knew that the families' behavior would be affected by the presence of an observer in the home, but because families had to give informed consent to having their behavior recorded, we could not avoid observer effects. Rather than try to record when people were unaware, we discussed how to help families habituate to observation so they could relax and behave naturally. We decided to put the observer in the home so family members could observe the observer. They could see what she was watching and writing, and they could ask questions and comment or explain. In one home, for example, an older child asked the mother during an observation, "Why does she keep writing when he's not doing anything?" The mother answered, "Because that's her job." At the end of the observation hour, the observer explained to the older child that it was important to know the details of everything the child did because that would probably be what he talked about later on.

We decided to start observing before the children began to talk so that families could get used to the observer, and we could establish trust and rapport. We also decided to record for 1 hour at a time because it is hard for people to maintain unnatural behavior that long. This is especially true of young children with very short attention spans. We had learned in preschools and child care centers that children's behavior is a reliable indication of how natural the adults are because children cannot pretend to be comfortable when adults are behaving in unfamiliar ways. We expected people to be on their "good behavior" while being observed; we assumed we were recording the "good behavior" that was natural for parents.

Defining "Everything"

Given that we wanted to record "everything" that went on in children's homes,[7] the first step was for the four future observers to agree on a definition of everything. The four observers started by watching videotaped parent–infant interactions and recording everything that transpired. After several such sessions, the observers decided to record only the behaviors of each person that were likely to be followed by a change in the other person's behavior. We assumed that behaviors that had no effect on what other people did were unlikely to contribute substantially to differences in vocabulary growth. In this way, we defined what the observers were to select from the ongoing stream of behavior. For example, they needed to attend not to a parent reaching for a washcloth but to the parent using a washcloth to wipe the baby's face, because the baby often reacted to the parent's action by pushing the parent's hand away.

When the four observers could agree on what to watch for, they could go back to the videotape, several times if necessary, and agree on a list of behaviors to which the child and parent reacted. They could agree, for example, that a parent reacted to a child's pointing to a toy by giving the toy and that the child reacted to the parent's giving the toy by taking the toy. When the observers had a catalog of behaviors they could agree that people tended to react to (e.g., pointing, giving), they could record those behaviors whether or not someone reacted. Observation could then focus on which of the children's early exploratory behaviors their parents and siblings were responding to, how often, and in what fashion.

26

Having agreed on the behaviors to record, the four observers began to observe real people, the infants interacting with each other and their caregivers in the Infant Center[8] in Lawrence, Kansas. At first the observers recorded for 10 minutes and then adjourned to compare their observations. Eventually they could observe for 1/2 hour and agree on 90% or more of what they recorded. But they had had to drop a number of behaviors from the list. For example, they could agree on looking and smiling only when the baby's face was turned to them; they had to define aggression in terms of crying by the infant who was hit because they could not agree that the baby who hit had intended any harm.

After the four observers could agree on 90% of what was going on during interactions in the Infant Center, they finalized a set of codes and observation procedures.[9] Then they began to observe real parents in real family settings, in the homes of two of the observers' friends who had infants. This led to adding new codes and redefining old ones. For example, a code was added for talk not addressed to the child, and proximity was redefined as present in the same room as the child. Although the original definition of proximity (within 10 feet of one another) would have added precision to the data, the importance of the precise distance did not seem commensurate with the difficulty of training four people to judge distance accurately while they were supposed to be focused on recording family and child activities.

During the 4 months of reliability observations in the two homes, as the observers developed and mastered observation methods and codes all four could agree on, plans were made for recruiting families. To study differences in vocabulary growth rates, we needed a range in demographics: We needed to recruit families different in size, racial background, and socioeconomic status (SES).

We decided to start when the children were 7–9 months old so we would have time for the families to adapt to observation before the children actually began talking. Finally, we wrote a one-page summary of the purposes and procedures of the research to send to prospective families, and we began recruiting.

Finding Participants

The first families we recruited came from personal contacts: friends who had babies and families who had had children in the Turner House preschool. We then used birth announcements to send descriptions of the study to families with children of the desired age. We were especially grateful for permission to present a description of the study at WIC meetings[10] because participants were prescreened for low income. We also used the state register of births to find unmarried mothers whose names were not included in public lists of births.

Families were sent or given the one-page description of the research and then contacted a week or so later to ask whether they were interested in participating. If they said they were interested, we scheduled an interview in the home. At the interview, the prospective observers described the study and its procedures in detail and asked for and answered parent questions. Especially stressed was our interest that parents "do what you usually do" when at home with the child so that we could see how children learn through casual interactions rather than through structured teaching sessions.

Two potential observers went to each interview. We knew that to maintain families in the study we would have to build rapport between the parents and the observers. If parents were to feel comfortable enough to behave naturally, they would need to be confident that they were not being judged or misunderstood. The more similar in outlook the family and observer were, the easier this would be for both of them. So, the one of the two observers who was the better match in terms of background and age was suggested for parent approval as the observer. After the informed consent form was explained and signed, we asked for demographic information and information about the child, and we scheduled a time for the first observation.

In recruiting, we had two priorities. The first priority was to obtain a range in demographics, and the second was stability—we needed families likely to remain in the longitudinal study for several years. A unique data set from a teenage mother recruited through WIC had to be discarded, for example, when her family moved her out of the city after 6 months of observations. Recruiting from birth announcements allowed us to preselect families. We looked up each potential family in the city directory and listed those with such signs of permanence as owning their home and having a telephone. We listed families by sex of child and address because demographic status could be reliably associated with area of residence in this city at that time. Then we sent recruiting letters selectively in order to maintain the ratio of child sexes in the study and the representation of socioeconomic strata.

After sending the recruiting letter, we telephoned the family during the day; after the third try we set the family name aside because few mothers who worked every day expressed interest in participating in the research. Also, we did not want to start out observing evenings and weekends. By the end of the study we were regularly doing so because many of the mothers went to

29

work after the children were 2 years old. We persisted in trying to contact a family only when the family represented a scarce demographic category such as higher SES African American. Once we got to the initial interview, every family consented to observation in the home.

We began observations in the home as soon as we recruited a family. We continued to recruit for 5 months, replacing five families who moved away or could not be reached to schedule the next observation. During this time we came to realize just how much time is needed for transcribing. When the observers no longer had 5 minutes to spare for recruiting, we decided to stop. At that point we had enrolled 50 families. Subsequently four families moved away, and four families missed enough observations that their data could not be included in the group analyses.

Real Families

For the 42 families who remained in the study, we have almost 2 1/2 years or more of sequential monthly hour-long observations in the home. The families included some in which the mother never worked outside the home and some in which the mother worked part time or full time on a variable schedule (as nurses do). In several families the mother worked nights or evenings while the father was at home. A number of mothers went to work full time after the study was underway; several went into home child care, and two started their own businesses. Mothers worked mainly in clerical jobs, although some were nurses, speech therapists, and food handlers. One mother was a bartender and another was a law student.

All but eight of the families were intact, and in all but one of the families the father or another adult male was regularly involved in daily life. Over the years of the study, there were only three intact families in which the observer never met the father. In nine families, observations were sometimes recorded when the sole caregiver was a grandparent or the father. Fathers worked as university professors, janitors, salesmen, engineers, in construction trades, or in offices. One father was a pastor and another was an airplane mechanic.

One way of summarizing demographics is to use socioeconomic status based on occupation (see Chapter 3, endnote 4, for the definition of socioeconomic status used in the analyses). On the basis of occupation, 13 families were upper SES, 10 were middle SES, 13 were lower SES, and 6 families were on welfare. There were African American families in each SES category, in numbers roughly reflecting local job allocations. One African American family was upper SES, three were middle, seven were lower, and six welfare families were African American. Of the 42 children, 17 were African American and 23 were girls. Eleven children were the first born to the family, 18 were second children, and 13 were third or later-born children. At the end of the study 19 of the mothers were either pregnant or had had another child; only three children were still only children. In 22 of the families the child had a younger or slightly older sibling who was always present during observations. (See Table 1 for family characteristics by SES group.)

Over the years of observing the everyday lives of the families, not only were fathers, siblings, grandparents, aunts, and uncles present during observations but also the parents' friends, the friends brought with them by

31

Table 1. Averages and (ranges) in family characteristics by socioeconomic (SES) group

Characteristic	SES group		
	Professional	Working-class	Welfare
Number of families	13	23	6
African American[a]	1	10	6
Girls	8	12	3
Number of observations	28 (27–30)	28 (23–30)	29 (28–30)
CA[b] at first observation	9 (7–11)	9 (7–12)	8 (7–9)
Number of siblings	1 (0–2)	2 (0–5)	2 (1–4)
Mother's age[c]	30 (22–35)	27 (18–36)	21 (19–24)
Father's age[c]	34 (26–46)	30 (20–45)	25 (21–31)
Mother working[d]	5	14	0
Mother's education[e]	16 (12–18)	13 (11–18)	12 (11–12)
Father's education[e]	18 (16–24)	13 (11–18)	12 (11–14)
Family income[f]	43 (25–68)	28 (9–64)	5 (4–6)
SEI score[g]	71.3 (57.9–88.3)	31.1 (17.6–48.1)	10.0 (10.0–10.0)[h]
Words per hour[i]	2,153 (1,019–3,504)	1,251 (143–3,618)	616 (231–947)

[a]*T* tests showed there was no significant difference in socioeconomic index (SEI) by race within the working-class families.

[b]Child's age in months.

[c]Parent reported age at the time the observed child was born.

[d]Mother was regularly employed full or part time during the period of the study.

[e]Number of years reported.

[f]Reported annual family income in thousands of dollars.

[g]Socioeconomic index from Stevens and Cho (1985). In families with the mother working, the SEI score is the higher of the two parent scores.

[h]Because the welfare parents were not employed, there was no listing in Stevens and Cho (1985), and we added 10.0 for persons unemployed.

[i]Words addressed per hour to the child between 13–36 months of age. Averages for individual parents are shown in Appendix A.

siblings and relatives, plus a variety of repairmen and salespeople. Each observation was scheduled for a day and time chosen by the parent; the parent was reminded the day before the observation and could reschedule it at any time. If an observation was cut short, as occasionally happened when a 1-year-old fell asleep, the observer went to the home again within the week to record the amount of time needed to make up the full hour. Whenever an observer went to a scheduled observation, she always recorded the family as she found it; she never asked whether she could come back another day when there were not so many people there.

The 42 families we observed for more than 2 years represented a broad spectrum of society. They were very different from one another in personalities and family lifestyles, but they were also like one another: They were all well-functioning families. In comparison to the typical family, perhaps, the parents were more confident of their parenting skills, more self-assured and comfortable about being observed; they were probably less transient than average and perhaps more traditional in their values. They chose to be observed at the times they and their children were feeling well and unstressed and so likely to display good behavior.

Starting Out

When observations began, families and observers could be equally uncomfortable. Our first task was to establish rapport and professionalism. We paid $5 for each observation; it served to mark the relationship as one in which both parties were working. (One parent said to her child at the end of the study, "Unemployed at age 3.")

Initially the observer stationed herself against a wall near the child. She remained immobile and removed her eyes from what the child was doing only if the parent spoke to her or began to interact with the child. The observers never interacted with the child. They followed the child to another room in the house only with parent permission. They watched only the child and never the interactions between other family members. Part of the consent form the parents signed had informed them that they could ask the observer to stop taping at any time, but only one parent ever did. To the extent that the observers could, they avoided recording family interactions not involving the child.

When scheduling the day and time for observation, most parents chose times when they could be occupied with routine activities. At first we saw lots of mealtimes with a parent feeding a highly engaged child in a highchair. Washing dishes and folding clothes were also frequently observed activities. In general, parents tended to arrange a predictable activity where the child was secure, and they could get chores done while periodically interacting with the child and casually observing the observer.

The observer felt most comfortable focusing entirely on the child, and thus the parent could see that watching the child was indeed the observer's only interest. This focus also enabled the observer to comment after the observation on the child's new learnings and on the fascinating modes of exploration that she had seen. Parents occasionally commented that having the observer in the home made them more aware of the child's skills and progress. Obvious to the parent was that the observer found the child utterly charming.

The observers never interacted with the children, but they did respond to parents' comments during observation. They tried not to encourage parents to talk to them during observations partly because it preempted talk to the child but also to avoid having to transcribe such talk. Instead they spent time talking to the parent after the observation. But the observers never gave advice even when asked, and they never said anything negative about the child or agreed if the parent did. They never commented on other children or families in the study even if the families knew one another. Even among themselves, the observers did not talk about or interpret what they saw families do.

Real Lives

In most cases the observer set up a schedule with the family to come at the same time every month so that the observations could be part of the family routine. Parents seemed to become quite comfortable with the observer; by the time the children were walking, most parents were inviting the observer to follow the child beyond the parent's presence. Although no parent was unaware that the observer was there, over time the observer tended to fade into the furniture. The observer was a silent, friendly, but not very interesting presence, someone who provided casual monitoring and a passive social audience for the child.

The match was good enough that all of the families let the observers continue to come even after the children entered the "terrible twos" and began challenging their parents with some highly inventive inappropriate behavior. Families felt comfortable enough that a parent occasionally left the observer alone with the children while the parent ran next door. One observer arrived to find that the usual four family members had four additional extended family members visiting for the hour. Another found herself observing the family children playing with flashlights in an unlighted garage. A third had to enlist the parent to stop the child from throwing rocks at her.

A positive result of the trust between parents and observers was that no family dropped out after the first year; most parents, if they could not be at home, called in advance to reschedule or directed the observer to the home of a relative who was caring for the child. The parents provided to the observers each month for 2 1/2 years the unique privilege of recording the everyday lives of real families raising children.

Reliability

Because we did not want to risk disrupting the naturalness of the observations or the rapport established with the families, we decided to keep the same observer in the home throughout the study and to assess interobserver reliability[11] in two other ways. First, regularly, for a majority of the tapes, one of the other observers independently transcribed a random section so that observers could get immediate feedback on the quality and consistency of their work. Second, every 6 months the observers returned to one of the families who had volunteered to accommodate four-way reliability observations during observer training. The four-way reliability observations served primarily as opportunities for the observers to recalibrate as the children developed and began talking. That the observers could continue to achieve high percentages of interobserver agreement assured them that they were generalizing the coding and transcription in identical ways.

All but nine of the families had the same observer every month for 2 1/2 years. Of the original four observers, one left after 8 months; she trained her replacement who left after 6 months. Bringing in a new observer is bad for a family who has to build rapport with someone new and bad for the data if the adjustment leads to a period of unnaturalness. Rather than spend time training another observer who might leave, we decided that one of the already-trained observers would take over the nine families, and we would hire a typist to do a preliminary transcription of tapes for the observer to correct and annotate. Of the three permanent observers, the two African American high school graduates observed 15 of the African American children; the white college graduate observed 25 white and 2 African American children. Each observer recorded the interactions of at least one family on welfare.

Writing It All Down

During each hour of observation, the observer carried a tape recorder and a clipboard; she focused on writing down what the child was doing, the materials the child contacted, and who was present and interacting with the child. She wrote down bits of dialogue so that when she transcribed the tape she could link events and utterances into interactional episodes. Observing the child and collecting the data was the enjoyable part of the research; the unpleasant part was creating a record from the observation that could be analyzed by computer.

Others have commented on how long it takes to transcribe 1 hour of tape, even into standard English orthography as we did, and with the proviso that we did not have to spell every word correctly at the time. It can take 8 hours to transcribe 1 hour of interaction between a parent and a child. Each additional person such as a sibling can add an hour to transcription. When several extra adults and children are present, there may be two or more conversations going on at once, and each must be listened to separately in order for it all to make sense.

We made a decision that we would use all the data we collected: We would not leave any tapes untranscribed. This meant getting each tape transcribed before going to the family home to record the next one. Accurate and efficient transcription depended not only on listening to the tape in conjunction with the contextual notes written in the homes but also on the observer's memory. The tape and the notes were used to reactivate the observer's memory of the situation as a whole; even after 10 years they can still do so.

When an observer transcribed a tape, it was like seeing a movie of the whole observation over again. The observer retained considerable peripheral knowledge about events and situations that the context notes served to signal and highlight. She could account for a sudden noise or other people's talk on the tape, for example, in terms of what was going on in the home that she had not been directly attending to at the time. But it was critical to capture this memory before the next observation created a new memory that would interfere with it.

Transcribing tapes is boring and incredibly tedious. Most of the novelty and all of the fun was had during observation; the only excitement the observers got from listening to the tape was confirming a new word or a new skill step for the child. Adult talk had to be transcribed three or four words at a time with frequent reviewing to check, for example, whether the adult said, "You wanna...?," or "D'you wanna...?" All the observers had the experience of writing an utterance they "heard" in the ambient talk on the tape, reading their notes, and then hearing an entirely different utterance. This led to the rule not to interpret what was said, or paraphrase, but to use the code CU (can't understand) if a word or utterance was not clear.

The burden of transcribing is so onerous that the observers soon learned strategies for regulating observations for ease of transcription: Do not encourage adult–adult conversation. Write down every word when someone turns on a mixer or a vacuum. Write a warning note when a child screams or begins banging a spoon on a pie plate. Point the microphone away from heaters, fans, and the television. The original recruitment letter asked that the television be off during observations but if a parent did not turn it off when the observer came to the home, the observer never asked the parent to do so; it was clear that in some families the natural situation always included a radio or television as a background to interaction.

Listening to Children

The critical aspect of observation was recording what the child said. This meant being as close to the child as possible and writing as much as possible of what the child said. The observers found everyone's speech easier to understand in the home when they could see what the speaker was doing; also, they had more experience adapting to variations in acoustics than to the variation in the range of timbres in recorded voices. (High ceilings always muffled speech; outside, the wind could simply blow the sound away.) The more an observer could note concerning what other people were talking about, the easier transcription was. It was critical to note whether or not talk was addressed to the child. If, for example, the observer heard someone say, "Stop that," or, "No no," it was important to code if it was for speech not addressed to the child; otherwise the observer would spend time going back over the tape and her context notes to be sure she had not missed something.

Writing down during observation what the child said was critical because much time was spent, in the best of circumstances, making sure that the child's early utterances, and the parent's responses to them, were completely and accurately transcribed. The observer tried to write what the child said while she was in the home, when she could see what the child was doing or looking at, and then confirm the clarity of the word on the tape before attributing a particular word to the child. If the parent did not confirm the child's word by repeating it or commenting on it, much time was spent reviewing the child's early words and asking a second observer to confirm their comprehensibility.

While the children were learning to talk, transcribing was interesting and challenging. Parents and observers alike were captivated by trying to understand what the children were trying to say. The parents used questions and tried out interpretations. The observers were the more fortunate in having the tape so they could listen again and again, slowing the tape down or speeding it up or enhancing the tone in order to clarify a child's speech. Transcribing could be punctuated by chuckles and calls for shared listening when a child pointing to butterflies in a picture was heard to say, "butt," "butter," "butterfly," or when a parent said to both the child and a sibling, "Leave it alone. Both of you," and the child responded, "Both of me?"

Finishing Up

By the last 6 months of observing, transcribing took twice as long and was not half as interesting. The children were so proficient in using language that their parents' most frequent comment concerned the child who "talks too much." To the parents, the observers said truthfully, "Not too much for the observational data." But in private the observers had to agree that, when the parent was not there to challenge the child to learn and elaborate, much of what highly verbose 2 1/2-year-olds have to say is not particularly compelling. A half hour of observation was spent, for instance, with a 2 1/2-year-old and her 4-year-old sister playing, one singing "She'll be coming round the mountain" over and over again and the other doing the same with "London Bridge."

The enjoyment of observing people's everyday lives and watching children grow and learn had its price: the endless time spent listening and re-listening to tapes, checking context notes and writing them in at the appropriate points, timing the 5 seconds of silence to separate interactional episodes, picking out the child and parent from all the other conversations going on at the same time, and then deciding how much was comprehensible in those other conversations the observer was not attending to. Beyond all this was having to take time out for continual reliability checks and the extra reliability observations that had to be transcribed and checked. We could earn one another's gratitude just by offering to put the page numbers on a transcription.

None of us took a day of vacation for more than 3 years—from our first observation until the last transcription was completed. We began to describe ourselves as being held prisoners by a longitudinal study, by the schedule of observations that continually produced tapes that had to be transcribed, and by the need to telephone or stop by a home over and over again for as long as it took to schedule the next observation. Parents' schedules completely determined ours: When parents took daytime jobs, our jobs began to take our evenings and weekends; when parents rescheduled, we were available at a moment's notice; after what might be a long drive to a home, we always waited 1/2 hour for a family to arrive for a scheduled observation before returning to the office. We developed intense gratitude toward those parents who never missed a scheduled observation, who telephoned in advance if there was any change in plans, who were understanding about equipment breakdowns, and who let the observer move around the house in a way that kept the microphone close to the child.

What kept us going was the continual springtime humanity displays in its children and our delight in rediscovering the world through children's enchantment with it. Added to this was the indescribable privilege of sharing the lives of a great many truly gracious people whom we would not have met in other circumstances. There was a kind of daily wonderment at seeing how other people live and how different each family's everyday life was from that of every other family. We saw that, at least in the Midwest, traditional American values remain robust. We spent 3 years observing friendly, considerate people who genuinely cared about their children; we ended up feeling above all a profound pride in American families and the promise of their future.

Into the Computer

As overwhelming as the task was to transcribe all the tapes by hand, we could do it; what we could not do was analyze the data by ourselves. Only a computer can handle the sheer quantity of data a longitudinal study generates. What we did not fully realize, however, was that in order to enable the computer to do its job, we would have to do 3 more long years of painstaking and even more boring work. We had 1,318 transcripts to process, each averaging some 20 pages, handwritten on both sides. Fortunately, we also had a highly creative and devoted computer programmer with whose help we designed a kind of assembly line of specialized tasks, ending in computer programs that turned each observation into numbers and dictionary words.

Before we could start, we had to decide on the database we wanted to produce. We had already defined and assigned number codes to many of the behaviors we wanted to count; during observations, for example, we used codes learned during training to note nonverbal behaviors such as pointing and touching. During transcription we had coded an interactional episode as ending if no one responded to a child or adult behavior within 5 seconds. Then the next behavior was coded as an initiation; the other person's behavior that reacted to it was coded as a response. Behaviors that intervened before the next response were coded as floorholding turns.

The goal of the longitudinal study was to discover relationships between family interaction patterns and vocabulary growth rates. Thus vocabulary needed to be a primary product in a form we could compare among all the families as well as to the data we had collected from the 4-year-old children studied at the Turner House Preschool. Therefore, we decided to code words into four categories: nouns, verbs, modifiers (adjectives and adverbs), and functors (pronouns, prepositions, demonstratives, articles). Special codes were assigned to proper nouns because so many of these were family-specific proper names; a family vocabulary could be artificially inflated, for example, just by a visit from extended family members. Another special code was assigned to

43

words we knew we would not want to compare across families or over time: animal and vehicle sounds (e.g., meow, beep-beep), swearing, foreign words (e.g., gesundheit), and private or coined words that were not listed in the dictionary we used to check and standardize spelling.

We also wanted to count how often children heard and said certain kinds of utterances over the time they were learning to talk. We defined and assigned number codes to, for example, whether an utterance was a sentence or a phrase and, if a sentence, the number of clauses it contained and whether it was a statement, a question, or a demand. We defined special codes for repetition, expansion and extension, and positive and negative feedback. Then we embarked on coding each utterance in each of the 1,318 hours of observation.

Assembling a Corpus

First on the assembly line was a high-speed typist who entered the utterances, with speaker and episode codes, onto an individual computer file coded with the date of the observation and the family. The next step involved a computer program that displayed each utterance to a coder who specialized in entering the part-of-speech codes. The program supplied codes for such high-frequency words as "you" and "go" and verified that the codes entered by the coder were acceptable types and neither too few nor too many. The coder checked each utterance against the raw transcript, corrected misspelled words, and entered words omitted, as did each person in the assembly-line process.

The next step involved a coder who entered codes that required looking at the data beyond the level of the individual utterance (e.g., to check whether an utterance was a repetition of a prior speaker) and prepared the data for the syntax program. We found that the computer program could use the part-of-speech codes to supply the syntactic code for about three fourths of all the utterances in an observation. The program supplied codes for such high-frequency utterances as "what's that?" and "I don't know." Then a syntactic code was proposed, which the operator either accepted or changed. For an utterance that contained no word coded as a verb, for example, the program proposed one of the phrase codes. For an utterance with a verb as the first word (e.g., "Give me"), the program proposed the code for an imperative. If the initial verb was an auxiliary (e.g., "Will you give me"), the program proposed the code for an auxiliary-fronted yes/no question with a future tense.

After the syntax program was run, the fully coded observation was submitted to a program that verified that all the codes had been accurately supplied such that the data were ready to process. One of the principal investigators ran the final check on each file and then ran the two programs that summarized each observation. The first program produced frequency counts for each code by episode type (routine care, mutual play, unstructured activity) for each of six speaker categories: child, parent speaking to the child, parent speaking to someone other than the child, other adults speaking to the child, other children speaking to the child, and others speaking to others.

The second program produced an individual dictionary for each of the six speaker categories. Each individual dictionary was indexed to a master dictionary that, at the end of the study, contained 15,000 words. As the program ran, the operator was given a final chance to change any misspelled or miscoded words. Once the data from all the families had been run, the master dictionary was decoded to list the frequency that each word had been recorded for each child in each family or in all the families. The most frequent word spoken to the children, for example, was "you"; the most frequent word spoken by the children was "I."

After all 1,318 observations had been entered into the computer and checked for accuracy against the raw data, after every word had been checked for spelling and coded and checked for its part of speech, after every utterance had been coded for syntax and discourse function and every code checked for accuracy, after random samples had been recoded to check the reliability of the coding, after each file had been checked one more time and the accuracy of each aspect verified, and after the data analysis programs had finally been run to produce frequency counts and dictionary lists for each observation, we had an immense numeric database that required 23 million bytes of computer file space. We were finally ready to begin asking what it all meant.

At Last

It took 6 years of painstaking effort before we saw the first results of the longitudinal research. And then we were astonished at the differences the data revealed (see Figure 2). While we were immersed in collecting and processing the data, our thoughts were concerned only with the next utterance to be transcribed or coded. While we were observing in the homes, though we were aware that the families were very different in lifestyles, they were all similarly engaged in the fundamental task of raising a child. All the families nurtured their children and played and talked with them. They all disciplined their children and taught them good manners and how

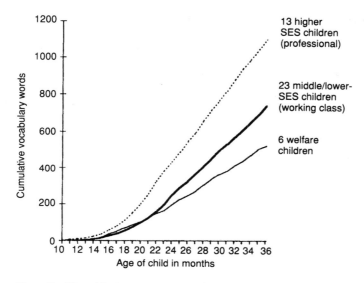

Figure 2. The widening gap we saw in the vocabulary growth of children from professional, working-class, and welfare families across their first 3 years of life. (See Appendix B for a detailed explanation of this figure.)

to dress and toilet themselves. They provided their children with much the same toys and talked to them about much the same things. Though different in personality and skill levels, the children all learned to talk and to be socially appropriate members of the family with all the basic skills needed for preschool entry.

Beyond this was the observers' side of the rapport established with the families. The only joy in the years of collecting and coding the data was being with the families. The empathy and depth of fondness we felt for the families arose from sharing their lives, seeing them as real people dealing with real children and real problems in the best ways they knew. Only when all the data were turned into numbers could we distance ourselves from the families and separate the world of parenting practices and vocabulary outcomes from the individual families and children we cared about so much.

When we saw the numbers, it was clear that the 6 years of hard labor was time well spent. We had collected, coded, and analyzed the data hoping to see differences in vocabulary growth rates. Now the observation summaries showed us the very differences we had set out to find (see Figure 2).

But now we had an hour of observation from every month since the children's first words and objective data that we could use to examine what was going on in the homes during the time that the children's vocabularies were growing.

Endnotes

1. Language development is an incredibly broad field of study because learning to produce and comprehend language involves integrating physical, social, and cognitive skills (see Fletcher & Garman, 1986). The early literature describing how children's performance changes over time and development (see Brown, 1973; Carmichael, 1954) has been succeeded by a wealth of studies concerned with children's developing knowledge of the meanings and rules of the language (see Bloom, 1993; Rice & Kemper, 1984; Smith & Locke, 1988). Largely left to psychologists are issues relating to what parents and children actually talk about and the impact on children of what parents tell them (Gleason, 1985).

2. The term "parenting" covers a lot of ground, including the kinds of physical and social environments parents provide (see Gottfried, 1984), affective relationships such as attachment (see Bretherton & Waters, 1985), and child-rearing practices such as the use of reasoning versus power assertion (see Baumrind, 1971; Maccoby & Martin, 1983). Methodological rigor leads such studies to focus on relationships between limited, well-defined sets of variables and child outcomes measured by tests of intelligence or psychological adjustment; Furstenberg (1985) discusses the lack of research that describes children as an inseparable part of an interactive family system that is continually changing as the child develops.

3. The most famous of such anthropological work is that of Margaret Mead (1928) on growing up in Samoa; more recent studies are those of Schieffelin and Ochs (1978) and Richman, LeVine, New, Howrigan, Welles-Nystrom, and LeVine (1988). The cross-cultural studies of Whiting and Whiting (1978) are equally fascinating as are the studies of the early lives of poor children in urban (Heath, 1983) and rural (Gazaway, 1969) America. Anthropological work integrates the child in the family but relies on the

observers' descriptions rather than on "real data on what happens" in the family (see Gleason, 1985, p. 277). Schieffelin and Ochs (1978) addressed issues concerning how cultural conditioning can influence observers' perceptions and interpretations of the interactions of others.

4. See the discussion by Zaslow and Rogoff (1981), in which they considered cross-cultural observations of interaction and how comparable performance during brief laboratory sessions is to what families routinely do at home.

5. We do have a considerable number of longitudinal studies of children's development, such as the Berkeley Growth Study (Bayley & Schaefer, 1964) and the Children of the National Longitudinal Survey of Youth (Chase-Lansdale, Mott, Brooks-Gunn, & Phillips, 1991), in which the data derived from tests and interviews. The Pennsylvania Infant and Family Development Project (Belsky, Gilstrap, & Rovine, 1984) used home observations to time sample certain parent behaviors, and the Bristol Study (Wells, 1985) put recording instruments in the home in order to collect data on children's language interactions. The difficulties of collecting longitudinal data were discussed by Wells (1985) and Capaldi and Patterson (1987), who encountered most of the same problems we did.

6. We are grateful to Dr. Peter Bentler, University of California at Los Angeles, for this suggestion.

7. An example of the amount of data collected by recording "everything" is the book *One Boy's Day* by Barker and Wright (1951).

Wagner (1985) concluded from a survey of the literature that children between the ages of 5 and 15 speak some 20,000 words per day, of which 2,500–3,500 are different words.

8. The Infant Center was a child care center operated by the Living Environments Group in Lawrence, Kansas, as a setting both for service to families and for empirical research into the management, care routines, teaching

techniques, materials selection, and environmental design that would ensure good, workable and economically viable out-of-home care for infants. For a complete description of the Infant Center, see Herbert-Jackson, O'Brien, Porterfield, and Risley (1977).

9. A copy of the complete observation and coding protocols is available on request from the authors.

10. WIC (Special Supplemental Nutrition Program for Women, Infants and Children) is the federal nutritional program run by state and local health departments. We are grateful to Rose Booth for permission to describe the research at WIC meetings in Kansas City.

11. Reliability was assessed at each phase. First, the observers were pretrained to 90% levels of interobserver agreement on coded behaviors. Second, during the observations a randomly selected section of 56% of the audiotapes was transcribed independently by a second observer. Finally, completed transcripts of four observations per child were checked by an independent listener and 22 randomly chosen observations were independently recoded to assess the reliability of the coding. Average percents of agreement were 93% or higher for all assessments. See also Chapter 6, endnote 3. For a more detailed description of the reliability measures, plus a description of attrition during and after recruiting, see Hart and Risley (1989).

CHAPTER THREE

42 American Families

❖ ❖ ❖ ❖

We had deliberately recruited a demographic range of families, from highly educated upper-SES families living in affluent suburbs to welfare families living in deteriorating neighborhoods, with most of the families in the middle. Differences in relative advantage were obvious in the homes, but material possessions and educational attainments were just part of the context of the observations, like gender and family size. The differences the observers noticed between families arose from the unique individuals in the families and how they interacted to create a characteristic lifestyle that was simultaneously distinctive as well as typical of well-functioning families. Our first task was to sift from all that made each family special what made families generally alike and different.

Similarities in Family Life

Raising children made all the families look alike. All the babies had to be fed, changed, and amused. As we went from one home to another we saw the same activities and lives centered on caregiving. We heard babies asked the same questions: "What are you doing?" and

53

"Are you full/hungry/wet/sleepy?"[1] Development made all the children look alike. The babies all babbled enthusiastically and explored everything they could reach by tasting, examining, shaking, pulling apart. If we saw a child in one home starting to say words, we knew we would see all the other children begin and all the parents joyfully take up repeating everything their children said. We saw all the children learn to eat with a spoon and get toilet trained. We saw them all begin to imitate, pretending to cook and drive a car.

We saw all the parents respond alike to developmental change. They all began to demand conformity, saying, "Use your spoon," "Say 'thank you'," "Put your shoes on," "Don't jump on the couch," "Put that in the trash," and "Do you have to go potty?" Much of what we heard the parents say was the same in all the families as they socialized their children to a common cultural standard. We would have been surprised if we had not seen such interaction between the children's increasing skills and the parents' rising expectations.

The parents were alike in ways that surprised us. They played games of stimulation involving lots of noises, laughing, and fondling, but they rarely played pat-a-cake or looked at books with their babies. They often left the babies alone to scoot around in walkers or to crawl around and try to pull themselves up on the furniture. They put things on the floor for the children to explore and then went away. Even from another room, though, they unerringly responded to the slightest sound of distress; even when their backs were turned they seemed to know when their children had runny noses or pants that were falling down. But they did not seem to notice their children's babbling, and they almost never imitated the sounds their children made.

We were astonished to see all the parents simply wait for their children to say words. They prompted, "Say 'bye'," or, "Say 'milk'," but they never coached or held out for a word; a parent waved a child's arm or gave a child a cup without seeming to expect words before the child began to say one or two words spontaneously. As if learning to talk was much the same as learning to walk, the parents just let their children practice babbling, apparently sure that words, like pulling themselves up, would appear in due time. When the children began to say words, we were delighted rather than surprised at how enthusiastically parents took up repeating their children's words and prompting the children to say more. Our surprise was with how naturally skillful all the parents were and the regularity with which we saw optimum conditions for language learning.

Same and Different in Everyday Parenting

Most impressive of all that the parents had in common was the continual and incredible challenge a growing child presents. Alike in all the families was the transformation of a complaisant babe in arms into a capricious toddler determined to test the limits proposed by society and built into material things. Parents had a year or so to bring a "little monster" into harmony with the family and culture without destroying a child's individuality. We saw parents regularly checking with friends and family about how to handle the sheer inventiveness of their children, wondering whether their immediate reactions were appropriate. Every day, it seemed, parents were coping with novel behaviors not discussed in all their books on child rearing.

What education and having several children gave parents was a bigger bag of tricks. The amount of freedom parents could give their children was directly related to the number and diversity of the strategies they could call on for anticipating, distracting, redirecting, and persuading their children. One parent, for example, had a junk drawer of miscellaneous utensils next to the sink where she washed dishes; the child stood on a stool and played and talked without reaching for the knives or the hot water the mother was busy with, and the mother never said, "No, no." Another parent told a child over and over, "Stop," as the child reached for an ashtray and the telephone but never offered the child a toy or an object the child could play with.

We saw how wide and yet narrow is the range of acceptable behavior in the contemporary cultures from which ordinary children emerge. Some babies spent the day carrying a bottle or a pacifier; none were allowed to suck their thumbs or fingers. Some toddlers were prohibited from playing with the kitchen pots and pans but not from tearing up their toys; all had age-graded, machine-made toys. Some children helped themselves from the refrigerator and ate breakfast as they walked around the living room still in the t-shirts they had slept in. We saw 2-year-olds brushing their own teeth (or eating toothpaste, according to their parents). Many of the children were put in time-out for disobeying; all but one mentioned spanking (past or prospective).

During the observations we saw each family as a very different mix of personalities, standards, and habits. We saw how readily children accepted what was usual, such as always getting up in the morning and occasionally falling down the stairs. What made a family normal was its stable and predictable ways of interacting. Everything said in the family was appropriate and entirely typical of how those particular parents and children usually talked and what they usually talked about. What they did was so natural for them in their immediate circumstances that it was only after all the observations were completed and we began coding the data, reading the successive transcripts from a family, that we could see the language of the family separate from the people and the circumstances of interacting.

Differences in Language Style

When we began to separate the language from the people, we were struck with the differences in the cultures being transmitted to children through the consistency of what their parents said. We could marvel at the politeness of a parent who said, "Why don't you pick the toys up for me?" and how reliably the child acted as if the parent had said, "Pick up the toys." We could wonder at the directive "You need to go look in your bedroom," introduced with the question "Do you think?", be surprised at how often children were told "You're silly," and ask why a parent threatens to whip a 2-year-old for trying to put a spoon in a shoe.

The parents' language seemed to reflect the number, variety, and flexibility of the behaviors they had for coping with the inventiveness of their children. Some parents, especially the college-educated and those with three or more children, appeared ever-assured and unhurried, amused but not surprised by what their children did. In the language data we saw a parent warn a child who started to throw cards, "Are you tired of playing this? Shall we stop playing?" and, when the child did not stop, offer an alternative, "Do you wanna play with your chalk or do you wanna get your pegs out?" We saw a parent give a child a choice, "Do you wanna do it by yourself or with my help?" and another parent try persuasion, "You did real good on your sandwich. Now see if you can eat up your carrot. Those are good for you. Can you eat your carrot up? That's the way. Let's finish your carrot because Grandma brought us some little boxes of raisins for dessert."

We saw all the children grow up to talk and behave like their families. Parents who said, "Move" and, "Shut up," had children who did the same; parents who explained, "You're gonna hafta play by yourself, O.K., because I'm trying to make lunch and I'm gonna hafta get the baby up," had children who also explained at length. We saw that language style was our best indicator of the culture being transmitted to children. The educated parents we observed, themselves the children of educated parents, were transmitting to the next generation an upper-SES culture with its care for politeness and distinctions in status. But we were impressed by how often the average families talked to their children in much the same way and wondered about the effects of television on cultural diversity.

Differences in Sociability

A difference between the families that we noticed during observations, and especially during transcription, was how much more some families talked than others. A family's language style affected the amount of language we recorded: explaining alternatives takes many more words than straightforward directives. Parents who explained more also asked more questions and encouraged their children to ask more questions that the parents then had to answer.

But the differences in amount of language were greater than simply differences in language style. Some families not only talked more at each opportunity but talked more often; they interacted more often and responded and initiated more often to their children. We saw some parents who talked continuously as they fed, dressed, or changed their babies and others who did so with only a few introductory and closing remarks. Moreover, the amount of talking the family did seemed to be part of the culture being transmitted to the child. After the children learned to talk and had all the skills needed to talk more than the family, they did not; the amount they talked stopped increasing as soon as they began to talk the amount typical of the family.

We were not surprised to find that some parents talked much more than others to their children. Wells reported similarly large differences in how much parents talked to their children in the Bristol study of 128 families in a range of SES groups and reported an average number of parent utterances addressed to 18-month-old children very similar to our average of 325 utterances.[2] Nor were we surprised to see how variable the amount of talking was in every family from month to month (see Figure 3). We had expected variability when we asked parents to just do what they usually did with the child and placed no restrictions on what activities could occur and how many other people could be present during observations. We had set out to record the real lives of families and describe children developing as part of an interactive, ever-changing family system. We were glad

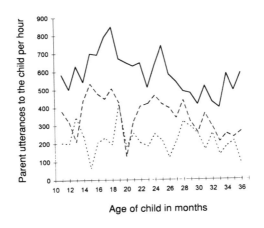

Figure 3.   A parent in a professional, a working-class, and a welfare family. Although the amounts varied from month to month, individual parents provided consistently different overall amounts of language experience to their children. (See Appendix B for detailed explanation of this figure.)

we had decided to get more data on fewer families so that we could use averages to distill from the continual variability of daily life the amount and style of interaction characteristic in a family and verify our findings using split-half reliability.

To the observers, the average differences the data revealed in the amount of talking that went on in the families merely corroborated their impressions. After only 6 months of observing, the observers could estimate the number of hours of transcription they would need to devote to a family and had begun trying to schedule their observations to alternate a "heavy" family with one in which there were frequent periods of silence. While the observers were in the homes, though, they were caught up in the individuality of the family; whatever went on partook of the style natural to the family. In some families interactions were naturally brief, an exchange of a few utterances followed by comfortable silence; other families demonstrated that people really can talk and listen simultaneously during conversation.

Influences on Differences in Sociability

The differences in how much parents talked to their children were so large and consistent that we looked for what might be influencing the amount of talking we recorded. We checked first for artifacts such as differences in the comprehensibility of parents' speech, time of day, and number of people present.[3] Having eliminated these we looked for family factors. We assumed that characteristics such as child gender and birth order, race, family size and SES, and parent employment and education would have an influence. We quickly eliminated gender as an influence: Correlational analysis revealed no differences in the amount of talk to boys and girls. And, as we expected from transcribing our observations in a demographic range of African American families, the influence of race was also quickly eliminated: Multiple regression analysis showed that after we controlled for SES there was no statistically significant association between race and amount of talk.

Having both parents employed made no difference to sociability. Some parents talked a lot even after a full day of dealing with customers or patients; other parents spent much of the day at home silently absorbed in soap operas. Most important, we saw no changes in the amount of talking that went on in families when mothers took jobs or quit the ones they had.

Birth order and family size made a difference in the allocation of talk but not in its amount. First-born children were recipients of nearly all the parent talk; the only competition was the telephone and an occasional visitor. But when a younger sibling was born, the allocation of talk became like that in the families with two children. The parents gave each child an equal share of a stable amount of family talk. The older siblings of the second-born children showed us the future of the first-born children we observed; as siblings were born, they too would apply their skills to regularly interrupting and preempting their parents' conversations with a new baby.

Family size made a difference because, to our surprise, more people present did not lead to more talking; each person just got a lesser share, including the baby. We were also surprised to see how seldom people other than the parents talked to the baby. Siblings and other adults interacted only briefly and rarely before the children began to talk about the same amount as the family. Having both parents available did not necessarily double the amount of talk to the baby; in the 27 families we observed in which both parents were sometimes home, the two parents talked more to the baby than did the one parent in 16 families and talked less in 11 families.

Socioeconomic status made an overwhelming difference in how much talking went on in a family. In the 13 families in which the parents were in professional and managerial occupations, the average number of parent utterances per hour when the baby was 11–18 months old and had barely begun to say words was 642, of which 482 were addressed to the baby. In the 10 middle-SES families in which the parents were working in offices and hospitals, the parents averaged 535 utterances per hour, of which 321 were addressed to the baby 11–18 months old. In the 13 lower-SES families in which the parents were working in construction, factories, and services, the parents averaged 521 utterances per hour, of which 283 were addressed to the baby 11–18 months old. In the 6 families on welfare, the parents averaged 394 utterances per hour, of which 197 were addressed to the baby 11–18 months old.

Defining Socioeconomic Status

The major difference we found between families was in the amount of talking that went on, and the family factor most strongly associated with amount of talking was SES. We decided to use SES groups for data analysis. Doing so would isolate the extremes in advantage and allow us to summarize the extraordinary differences we saw in the lives of children at those extremes and to compare them to our prior data from the professors' children and children from families in poverty.

Using a list of occupational codes,[4] we assigned each family the number that corresponded to the parent's job. In families in which both parents were employed, we assigned the family the higher of the two numbers. We added a number for those without a listed occupation (unemployed/welfare recipients). SES based on occupation was strongly associated with mother's years of education ($r = .73$), with the educational level of the household (both parents' years of education) ($r = .86$), and with reported family income ($r = .69$).

Examining the Consistency of Differences Among Families

Finding a strong association between amount of talking and SES did not surprise us; a number of prior studies had reported that higher SES parents talked more to their children.[5] But we needed to assure ourselves that the SES groups were consistently different in amount of talking and that, despite the month-to-month variability in the naturalistic data, the families remained consistent in typical amounts over the years of observation. We had heard the observers' comments as they transcribed the data, checked the observers' accuracy with reliability assessments (see Chapter 6, endnote 3), and seen the differences in the size of the files when we coded them. For further assurance we turned to statistics and an independent measure.

Amount of Time Interacting

We examined independently the actual amount of time per hour families spent interacting with their children across the months their children were learning to talk[6] (see Figure 4). The average family spent 28 minutes of an average hour interacting with the child; 12 minutes interacting with people other than the child; and, to the astonishment of the observers, an average of 20 minutes per hour not talking at all. Before the children were saying more than occasional words, the average family spent 23 minutes of an average hour interacting with the child; during the time the children were learning words most rapidly, the average family spent 30 minutes of an average hour interacting with the child; and after the children had learned to talk, the average family spent 29 minutes of an average hour interacting with the child.

The upper extreme in sociability was a higher-SES family that spent an average of 42 minutes per hour interacting with a child who was not yet saying more than a few words, an average of 48 minutes per hour during the time the child was learning words most rapidly, and an average of 55 minutes per hour interacting with the

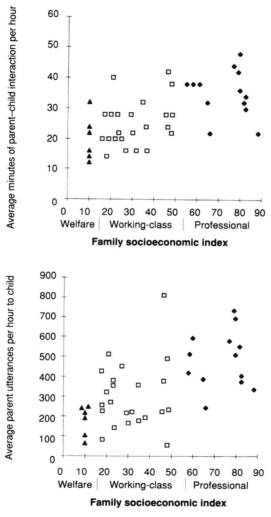

Figures 4 and 5. Each symbol shows an individual parent. Overall, the higher the social class of the parent, the more time and talk their children received. (See Appendix B for detailed explanation of these figures.)

child who had learned to talk. The lower extreme was a welfare family that spent an average of 7 minutes per hour interacting with a child not yet saying more than a few words, an average of 17 minutes per hour during the time the child was learning words most rapidly, and an average of 20 minutes per hour interacting with the child who had learned to talk. The child in the higher-SES family consistently got three times more experience with language and interaction than the child in the welfare family. In addition, in contrast to the child in the higher-SES family, the child in the welfare family was interacting with a sibling, not the parent, in 1 out of every 4 minutes of family interaction before, during, and after learning to talk.

Amount of Talk

We compared the amount of time per hour that each family spent interacting with the child (see Figure 4) to the average number of utterances per hour that the parent addressed to the child (see Figure 5) in order to verify the relationship between the two measures. The average number of utterances for all 42 parents was 341 utterances to the child per hour. The parents in the professional families addressed an average of 487 utterances to the child per hour in contrast to the average of 178 utterances addressed to the child by the parents in families on welfare, and the average of 301 utterances addressed to the child in the 23 working-class families.

To assure ourselves that individual families did not change markedly in relative rank over time, that no family that seldom interacted in the first months of observation was observed interacting frequently during the last months, we separated the data into blocks as small as 3–4 months and as large as 8–9 months and ran correlations between the blocks.[7] Correlations were .70 or better for parent and child turns and utterances across blocks of data. Paired *t* tests verified that the mean number of utterances recorded for individual families did not vary significantly across blocks of 8 months.

Split-half reliability showed us both the consistency with which the families separated into SES groups and the consistency of the amounts of talk characteristic within those groups over the 2 1/2 years of observation. When we split the corpus and compared the number of parent utterances recorded in the even-data months to the number recorded in the odd-data months, the correlations showed that differences in the relative sociability of the SES groups remained astonishingly stable across observations (see Figure 7). The split-half reliability also verified that changes in amounts of talking corresponded to changes in the amount of time families spent interacting with their children (see Figure 6).

Observing Differences in SES

We could see differences at the extremes in advantage, but both in the data and in our observations, the variability of the 23 "ordinary" families, those working-class by SES, made it almost impossible to characterize them as a group. Some families were far more sociable than others. Some were house-proud while others spent their money on vacations. A family starting its own business sacrificed on both. Some parents stressed academic achievement; others seemed more interested that their children have friends. We saw families who appeared intent on moving their children to a higher SES and families apparently enjoying having attained middle-class status.

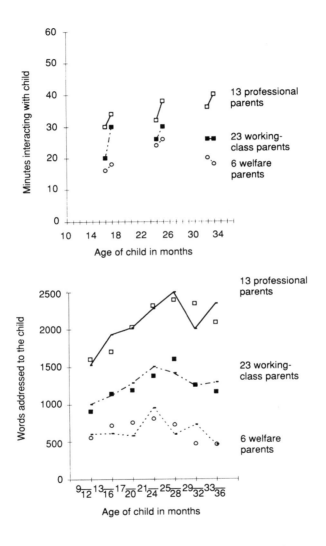

Figures 6 and 7. The differences between social classes in the time and talk their children received were consistent across the children's early years. (See Appendix B for detailed explanation of these figures.)

Remarkable about the upper-SES families was how busy they were—even parents who were employed volunteered time to church, school, and community activities. Parents at home all day were hardly isolated; they seemed so regularly to be talking on the telephone. Their children seemed to spend part of most days on the road, visiting friends, going shopping, or taking siblings to special activities. The children watched children's television programs such as *Sesame Street*; they had rooms of their own full of toys and books. Their parents spent time coaching them in how toys work and how puzzles fit together and involved them in helping prepare meals or sort clothes.

Remarkable about the welfare families was their isolation. In single-parent families without a telephone or a car, the parents could be virtually cut off from opportunities to talk with other adults. Those among the welfare families who lived in public housing projects, with all their dangers and drugs, at least had neighbors close enough to drop in. Families too poor to live in public housing put their children through successive moves from one small deteriorating dwelling to another. Often, the parents of parents on welfare seemed more critical of the family lifestyle, and less willing to help even when they could, than were other parents' parents. For some parents, their closest and most interesting friends seemed to be the characters on soap operas.

Particularly striking among the welfare parents was their resilience and persistence in the face of repeated defeats and humiliations, their joy in playing with their children, and their desire that their children do well in school. They could spend an hour on a bus holding a feverish child and wait longer than that in a public health clinic. They spent their scarce resources on toys for their children (though one parent said, "I don't know why. She just tears them up."). But these parents did not take the bus to the zoo, or turn the television to *Sesame Street*, and they did not talk to their children very much.

The Impact of Differences in Sociability

We found that characteristics such as the gender of the child, birth order, family size, and parent employment affected the allocation of family talk but not its amount. Children learning to talk, new babies being born, changes in jobs or residence, and other substantial changes in family life had only small effects on the amount of talking in the homes relative to the large and stable differences among the families.

We saw that these differences between families in amount of talk were so persistently characteristic of ongoing family life that they added up to massive differences in the children's cumulative experience with language. During the 8 months that the children were 11–18 months old, before they had begun to say more than a few words, the average number of utterances the parents addressed to the children was 325 per hour. The range, however, was from a parent who addressed an average of 793 utterances per hour to an 11–18-month-old child to a parent who addressed an average of 56 utterances per hour. When the children were 29–36 months old, parent utterances per hour ranged from 34 to 783. The amount a parent talked to a child during the first 8 months of observation was strongly associated with the amount the parent talked to the child at 3 years of age ($r = .84$).

The consistency we saw in family amounts of talk has grave implications. In an average 14-hour waking day, a child spoken to 50 times per hour will hear 700 utterances; a child spoken to 800 times per hour will hear more than 11,000 utterances. Given the stability in family styles that we observed, it is staggering to think of what 365 similar days in a year would produce in terms of cumulative experience with language: exposure to 250 thousand utterances versus 4 million utterances. When we consider differences in the probable content of those utterances, the implications for cumulative experience become yet more staggering.

We saw differences in how much parents talked to their children associated with differences in all the other relative advantages conferred by SES. At the extremes in advantage we saw the consistency and magnitude of the differences in home environments and early experiences we thought separated the daily lives of professors' children and children from impoverished families. Yet, despite those differences, all 42 children learned to talk. All the parents had apparently provided whatever amount of experience was necessary for the children to become effective users of the language. The family experience that gave rise to differences in rates of vocabulary growth must lie beyond whatever was essential to basic competencies. We needed to seek the aspects of everyday parenting that might be contributing to differing rates of vocabulary growth.

Endnotes

1. Quotation marks around parent statements indicate that we are quoting verbatim from actual family data.
2. Wells (1985) described the Bristol Language Development Study in England in which the speech of 128 children from a range of socioeconomic strata was recorded over a period of 3 1/2 years.

   Recordings were made in the home once every 3 months; the child wore a microphone, and a recorder automatically switched on for 90 seconds at 24 randomly selected times between 9 A.M. and 6 P.M. The same evening a researcher listened to the recording with the parents, who provided the context of the child's utterances and interpreted what the child said if necessary. Wells (1986) reported a number of findings similar to ours: Parents talked more to first-born children; other children rarely talked to children less than 2 years old; some parents addressed more than six times as many utterances to the child per observation than did others; and for some children as many as one third of 18 random samples throughout a day contained no speech at all.
3. The observers used the abbreviation CU (can't understand) to indicate any utterance or part of an utterance they could not hear or understand well enough to transcribe accurately. We calculated the percentage of CU utterances in all parent utterances. An average of 94% of parent speech was fully comprehensible; the range by family was from 79% (one family) to 98% (four families). In only three families was less than 90% of the parent's speech comprehensible.

   We listened to six tapes from each family early, in the middle, and late in the 2 years of observations and noted at 30 randomly spaced instants whether or not we heard someone talking. (See this chapter, endnote 6, for the specific methods used.) For these six tapes we also listed the time of day and the number of people present.

The six tapes included observations recorded at all times of the day from 8 A.M. to 6:30 P.M. Someone was heard talking an average of 40 minutes per hour; the number of minutes ranged from 34 (from 10:30 A.M. to 12 noon) to 44 minutes (from 4:30 P.M. to 6:30 P.M.). Seventy percent of the tapes were recorded before noon; talking was heard an average of 38 minutes. Thirty percent of the tapes were recorded between noon and 6:30 P.M.; talking was heard an average of 40 minutes. Minutes of interacting with the child varied unsystematically, averaging 26 minutes before noon and 30 minutes after.

The six tapes included observations recorded when 1–7 people were present in the home. Of these tapes, 77% were recorded when 1–3 people were present; talking was heard an average of 40 minutes. A total of 23% of the tapes were recorded when 4–7 people were present; talking was heard an average of 38 minutes. Number of minutes that talking was heard ranged from 36 (5 people present) to 44 (7 people present). Minutes of interacting with the child declined with each additional person present, from 34 minutes when 1 person (the parent) was present to 22 minutes when 7 people were present.

4. We assigned each family a number according to the occupation reported by the parent. We used the socioeconomic scores for the 1980 census occupational classification scheme based on the income and educational attributes of the total labor force, as listed in Stevens and Cho (1985). Parents were asked to report both mother's and father's occupation; in all cases, the parent's description of occupation tallied with the observer's knowledge of the parent's job.

5. Numerous studies of the effects of home environments on early cognitive development were presented in Gottfried

(1984). These studies showed, as did ours, more talking by higher-SES parents and no association between race and cognitive outcomes when families were equated for SES.

6. We listened to six tape recordings on each family early, in the middle, and late in the 2 years of observations and noted at 30 randomly spaced moments whether or not we heard someone talking. Using the transcript, the listener coded what she heard either as talk between other people or talk during interaction with the observed child. Silence was counted only when there was no interaction noted on the transcript; when voices were not heard because the instantaneous sample occurred during a pause within or between utterances, this was counted as interaction. Among the findings from listening to the tapes was that the television was on an average of 24 minutes of each hour and that the parent was not in the same room as the child an average of 10 minutes of each hour.

Reliability was assessed by having two listeners note on eight randomly chosen tapes simultaneously but independently whether someone was heard talking. The independent listeners agreed on whether voices or silence occurred on 97% of the momentary samples; they agreed on the exact word or pause in the transcript on 93%.

7. The means, ranges, standard deviations, and correlation coefficients for 10 measures of parent behaviors between 8-month blocks of data are shown in Hart and Risley (1992).

CHAPTER FOUR

Everyday Parenting

◆ ◆ ◆ ◆

W e had undertaken the longitudinal study to find out what was happening to children at home, both at the extremes in advantage and across the full spectrum of American families. We saw that, despite how strikingly different the families were in how much talking and interacting typically went on in the home, just socializing during everyday activities was sufficient for all the children to learn to talk by age 3. But at the extremes in economic and educational advantage we saw differences in rates of vocabulary growth similar to those we had seen in our preschool research (see Figures 1 and 2). These differences in rates of vocabulary growth suggested that there were important differences in what was going on within and across families as parents just socialized with their children.

Like other child development professionals, we assumed that some experiences are of higher quality than others in terms of their effects on children's learning. Some experiences are more developmentally important; some experiences are better adapted to children's current skill levels and are more helpful, informative, or challenging to growth. Based on our interpretation of the extensive literature concerning aspects that lend quality to home environments, parent–child interactions, and child rearing, we had in our prior work[1] defined 10 parenting variables and used a principal components analysis to cluster the variables into three factors. Regression analyses showed that two of the factors, the amount of parenting per hour and the quality of the verbal content associated with that parenting, were strongly related to the subsequent IQ score of the child.

Now we needed to describe more specifically what we saw parents saying and doing that seemed to add quality to everyday interactions. As with our impressions about the stability of a family's style of interacting, we came away from our observations with impressions concerning what made some interactions, in every family, more memorable than others as occasions for teaching and learning. We selected examples of these memorable interactions and used them as a basis for describing the parent behaviors that seemed to make these interactions higher in quality ("better") than others in terms of their developmental importance to language learning.

To ground subsequent discussions of quality features and of the categories of significant family experience we derive in Chapter 7, we present verbatim a series of examples from the observations. We include examples from the full range of the 42 families to illustrate that we did see quality interactions in every family, although considerably more often in some families than in others. The examples were also chosen to illustrate how quality is embedded in the casual socializing families do. Because the examples illustrate quality interactions, all show parents' "good behavior"; none of the parents, though, would have considered the particular interactions in the examples to be exceptional in terms of what they usually did with their children.

We characterize the examples using the statements the observers made to summarize their impressions of what parents did that added quality to interactions: "They just talked," "They listened," "They tried to be nice," "They gave children choices," and "They told children about things." We add a final example to illustrate one further impression of what parents did: They passed their interactional style on to the next generation.

They Just Talked

We saw quality added to interactions when we saw parents talking to their children beyond what was necessary to manage or provide care. Sometimes parents appeared to talk solely to engage with their children. They rambled on, commenting on whatever they were doing, and speaking for the child if necessary to maintain the semblance of a conversation. This seemingly aimless talk was especially noticeable when parents were talking to infants who were still acting as a receptive audience. Interactions could resemble parallel play, with the parent focused on washing dishes or putting on a shoe and with the child focused on exploring toys or trying to button a shirt. Parent and child remained intimately involved with one another, linked through a loose social bond of talk in which words were used less to organize conversation or communication than to create and sustain social closeness.

Talking for Sociability

The mother is not interested in conversation (note the infrequent questions) but in keeping the child cooperative and distracted. The mother could change the baby in silence; she talks for sociability, using words as an accompaniment to actions. Note how informative the mother is and how diverse her language is when she is not trying to prompt the child to respond or understand.

> The mother puts Kendra (9 months) on the changing table, saying, "Oh, it's leaking out of the side. Oh, that's a wet diaper." Kendra wriggles, babbling. Her mother says, "Stay," and then, "Oh, how about playing with daddy's keys?" She gives the keys to Kendra and then comments, "Gonna take you just about as long as it takes me to get you changed to figure out which one of those keys you wanna put in your mouth." The baby begins to babble as her mother continues, "By that time I'll take them away from you. What? Those are keys. Keys. Daddy's keys. He didn't drive this morning. No, let's not put them in our mouth, O.K.? They're good to look at but they're not good to chew on."

Talking to Stay Involved

Even as the mother is busy doing her work she remains involved with the child through casual talk about both their activities. Note how the mother follows the child's shifting attention by naming and describing and how spontaneously she alternates between addressing short, simple labels to the child and exposing the child to the mature language of adults (e.g., the metaphor of an obstacle course). Also notice how alert the mother is to a minor infraction when the child bends the card but how nice she is. She does not say, "Don't," or snatch it away, but she does mention it.

> Andrea (11 months) is playing with picture cards strewn on the floor; her mother is sorting pears at the kitchen counter. The mother says, "Let's see." Andrea begins to babble, holding out a card to her mother as her mother continues, "I wish some of these pears were good enough for me to keep. But I don't think any of them are.

So I'll just have to get some others for you." She turns to the child saying, "You like pears, don't you? Oh, are you trying to give me the camel?" Andrea's mother takes the card, saying, "Thank you. You know what? I'm going to put the camel right here so you can see the camel." She props the card against the stove.

Andrea gets the card and, babbling, inserts the card between oven and broiler. Her mother says, "Oh, you got the camel? You're bending the card. Can you be careful with it?"

Andrea crawls away and gets another card. Her mother says, "Did you find some more cards?" Andrea babbles and her mother names, "That's a zebra. Zippy zebra is what it says. Does that one sound like a horse? I don't know if it sounds like a horse or not. We know how a horse sounds, don't we? A horse goes. . . ." The mother makes neighing sounds; Andrea babbles and gets the box the cards were in.

Andrea's mother says, "Can you put your cards back in the box? Huh? Box. That's a tag. I don't think you can probably get that off. I think it's stuck pretty tight. Oh Andrea, sometimes I feel like my house is an obstacle course. As soon as you can walk we're gonna start making a game out of picking things up and putting them away, aren't we? Probably should start that already now. Except you think it's a game to pull them back out, don't you?" Andrea babbles, reaching for the cardboard center from an empty roll of paper towels. Her mother says, "What are you going after?"

They Listened

We saw quality added to interactions when we saw parents listening to their children beyond what was necessary to care for and educate them. Sometimes parents seemed to casually undertake the role of receptive social partner; they interrupted what they were doing to focus entirely on whatever their children had to say regardless of how repetitive, uninformative, or immature it might be. The parents seemed unconcerned with devising informative or challenging responses. They seemed to know that simply a moment of their exclusive interest, a comment, or a repetition of the child's utterance would suffice as an invitation for the child to continue.

Listening to Add Information

This mother is willing to do most of the conversational work in order to mediate an experience for her child. The mother responds to what the child is concerned about rather than to what the child actually says; she makes her interest in the child's topic clear by never commenting on the form or clarity of his utterances.

> Mother and Pete (35 months) are watching *Batman* on TV. Pete initiates, "Why they have hats on their heads?" His mother says, "Because they're in the army." Pete says, "And they are girls army." His mother says, "Girls can be in the army too." Pete says, "No." His mother says, "You know the lady that rides with Dad sometimes. She's in the army with Dad. And she's a girl." Pete says, "And they don't have hats on." His mother says, "Well they don't always wear their hats when they go to the army. But they have one. Like Dad has one."

Listening to Encourage Commenting

This parent is interacting with her child by taking the role of a receptive audience. Note how slowly the parent lets the lesson develop, guided by the child, and how undemanding she is, ready to keep the exchange going simply by repeating, and thus confirming the child's statements.

> Claire (24 months) is standing at her bedroom window looking into the yard. She points and says, "There see robin, red." Her mother confirms, "Yes, red."

After watching for a few minutes, Claire initiates again, "Mom, robin." Her mother says, "Yeah that's a robin." Claire says, "Bird robin." Her mother says, "Because he has a red tummy, huh?" Claire says, "Yeah. Sick. Sick." Mother says, "No he isn't sick. That bird's fine. He isn't sick." Claire says, "Tummyache," and her mother says, "No he doesn't have a tummyache. He has a red one. See the red on his tummy?" Claire says, "I see it." Her mother says, "Yeah that's where the robin is red, isn't it? On his tummy."

Two minutes later Claire initiates again, "Mom, robin." Her mother says, "Yeah, is he still standing there?" Claire says, "Red. Red right here," reaching to her waist. Her mother says, "Red robin." Claire says, "Shirt," and her mother says, "Red tummy." Claire says, "Red tummy."

A minute later Claire initiates again, "There a robin. Robin. Tummy red. See there?", and begins to play at unsnapping her belt.

Listening to Prompt Elaboration

This parent is a social partner in her child's pretend play. She is prompting and encouraging her child, but she lets the child control the course of the activity.

Rosa (24 months) is playing with a set of keys and an ashtray. When her mother interrupts to pull up Rosa's pants, Rosa says, "Let me cook." Her mother says, "Let you cook what?" Rosa says, "Cook this," and her mother asks, "What you cooking?" Rosa says, "This." Her mother asks, "What's that?" Rosa says, "My cooking," and her mother says, "It has to be something you cooking. What you cooking?" Rosa says, "This," and her mother says, "But what is it? What kind of food is it?" Rosa says something incomprehensible and her mother interprets, "Chicken?" Rosa says, "Uh-huh. Cook that chicken. I want this." She takes a piece of paper from the table. Her mother says, "It ain't nothing but paper." Rosa says, "Let me cook." Her mother says, "Let you cook what? You cooking but you don't know what you cooking." Rosa says, "I cooking." Her mother says, "Okay."

Rosa says, "This," and her mother asks, "Did you get some pop for dinner?" Rosa says, "Get that here for your dinner," and holds out the paper. Her mother says, "I don't want that dinner." Rosa says, "Eat that," and her mother says, "I don't eat paper. I thought you was cooking something." Rosa says, "I cooking. I put it in the icebox." Her mother says, "You put it in the icebox? Where's the icebox?" Rosa points to the kitchen, "In there." Her mother says, "You can't put that in the icebox."

Rosa pretends to shake something onto the paper and her mother says, "What you putting on it?" Rosa's 6-year-old brother suggests, "Ketchup." Rosa says, "Ketchup. Me put some ketchup on it." Her mother repeats, "You put some ketchup on?" and Rosa's brother asks, "Is it a hamburger?" Rosa says, "No," and her brother asks, "What cooking?" Their mother says, "She don't know what she cooking. She just cooking."

They Tried to Be Nice

We saw quality added to interactions when we saw parents trying to be nice even as they corrected their children. However strict or lenient parents typically were, they all had to discourage their children's inventiveness at times; none hesitated to tell their children "No" and "Don't." But we saw parents trying to avoid telling their children that the children were "bad" or wrong. They moved the children or took something away without saying anything. They suggested or provided alternatives that would engage the children in activities the parents could then encourage. Even when they had to criticize or prohibit behavior they tried to do so gently and provide a reason.

Trying to Be Nice When Enforcing a Rule

This parent is being both nice and strict. Note how many alternatives the mother has to criticizing or saying, "Don't." She names the "right" behaviors she wants to see rather than commenting on her children's misbehavior. She counts to three so that the children have time to "choose" to do as she tells them. She calmly insists, responsive but undistracted, on the rule that done means put away. She has established a consequence, sending the child to her room. Note toward the end of the interaction how she cuts short her question, adapting to the degree of cooperation she is getting at the moment, and gives the children a directive instead of a choice. And still she is polite ("Please") and appreciative ("Thank you").

Their mother enters the bedroom where Jaron (32 months) and his sister Julie (4 years) are hiding under the bed. The mother initiates, "Guys, I'm gonna say three and then you better be out from under the bed. One. Two." Both children emerge and their mother adds, "I don't want you staying under there, O.K.? If you're done with the doctor's kit please put it away, O.K.?" Jaron says, "Mom, where can I hide in?" His mother says, "Well you really don't need to hide anywhere. If you're done with the doctor's kit I want you to pick it up, O.K.? And then we'll find someplace else, O.K.?" Jaron says, "You want me to do the table?" His mother says, "Well pick up the doctor's kit first, O.K.?"

Julie interrupts, "I don't have to pick mine up." Her mother tells Julie, "You do too," and Jaron adds, "You too." Julie shakes her head and her mother says, "All right Julie you can just go in your room. I'm not gonna play games with you today. Go help him pick up the doctor's kit now." Julie says, "No," but helps anyway.

Jaron initiates, "Mom, we did." His mother says, "Thank you. Are you gonna put. . . . Put the box away now. Take it in and put it in the playroom, O.K.?" As Julie does this, her mother says, "Thank you. Thank you very much guys."

Trying to Be Nice When Prohibiting Exploration

This parent is benefiting from having been nice when she had to correct the child in the past. The child calls to tell her that he is embarking on exploring an object that has been forbidden in the past. Note that the parent tells the child what to do right and gives him affirmative feedback when he does. She never criticizes him; she talks about the table, the toy, the relationship between them, and what she wants without ever suggesting that she considers the child, or even the child's behavior, "bad."

The mother is in the kitchen filling the sink to wash dishes. Larry (33 months) takes his toy to the living room and begins to run it on the coffee table.
He says, "That's my motorcycle," and makes corresponding engine noises. He calls, "I got on your table, Mommy." From the kitchen, his mother answers, "You have a new table?" Larry replies, "Yeah, right here on my old table." Larry's mother comes to the living room and says, "Oh, I don't know. Larry, I don't want that to go on that one." Larry says, "That motorcycle. That's motorcycle, Mommy." His mother says, "That's gonna scratch my table. That has to go on the rug." Larry says, "That broke that." His mother agrees, "Oh, look what it did" Larry grunts, and his mother repeats, "That'll scratch my table. You can take it out on the kitchen floor with you. No, Larry, it'll scratch the table." Larry runs the toy on the rug, saying, "I do right here." Larry's mother says, "Oh, that's fine. Or you can bring it out here to the kitchen on the floor." She returns to the kitchen, and Larry, making engine noises, begins to run the toy on a stack of puzzles.

They Gave Children Choices

We saw quality added to interactions when we saw parents asking before demanding compliance or more mature behavior from their children. Parents avoided criticisms and commands by asking children to agree or disagree that what the children were doing was kind or appropriate. Even when the children clearly had no choice but to do as asked, parents offered the children an opportunity to say yes or no. They involved the children in decisions by giving the children a chance to voice a counterargument, an alternative, or an excuse.

Giving Choices as a Reminder

To remind the child of the appropriate behavior after toileting, this parent first models the yes/no question (the choices) that the child should say to herself in the future before she leaves the bathroom. Then the parent models the yes/no question the parent will ask. When the child chooses incorrectly, her mother asks again and continues to prompt until the child makes the correct choice.

Lynn (32 months) goes to use the toilet while her mother waits in the bedroom. When Lynn returns (no sounds of flushing heard), her mother asks, "Are you gonna flush it? Did you flush the toilet?" Lynn says, "No." Her mother says, "Would you go and flush it then?" Lynn does not answer, and her mother says, "Would you please go flush the toilet?" Lynn walks slowly back and flushes the toilet.

Giving Choices as Instruction

This parent is giving her child choices as (mostly ineffective) prompts for appropriate behavior. How much easier it would have been for the mother just to stir the yogurt herself and sit the child at the table rather than spend the time to guide the child to take the responsibility. Note the affirmative feedback for the appropriate behavior that occurs beyond the mother's immediate supervision, the importance the mother accords the behavior, and the hint that the mother would appreciate the child trying to produce it at the moment.

Corrine (34 months) comes to the kitchen and opens the refrigerator, saying, "Me get some yogurt. We got kinds of yogurt. Kinds of yogurt." Her mother says, "What kind you want?" and Corrine answers, reaching, "This kind." Her mother says as she gives Corrine the carton, "What kind is that?" Corrine says as she takes the carton, "That cherries," and, pointing, "Cherry, cherry, cherry." Her mother says, "You want your blue spoon? Or this spoon?" Corrine says, "I open it. That." Her mother says, "O.K.", and Corrine says, "That spoon," and takes one from her mother who asks, "You wanna sit up at the table?" Corrine says, "Have this right here."

Her mother offers, "Want me to stir it up for you?" Corrine says, "Let's sit right here," and begins to eat where she stands. Her mother makes her suggestion more specific, "You don't think you'll spill it?" Corrine says, "No," and her mother says, "Your teacher at playschool says that you eat so . . . that you're so careful when you eat and you're not messy at all. Is that right?" Corrine says, "Uh-huh," and her mother continues, "I was glad she told me that you did so well."

Corrine says, slurping from the spoon, "Yum yum yum yum." Her mother says, "Don't play with it though now. It's gonna go over the side, Corrine." Corrine whimpers, "I'm trying to take a big bite." Corrine's mother moves Corrine's hand, demonstrating, "Well here's one of the things you can do is you could brush along the side like that. There, then it won't come off on the floor. Why don't you sit up on your chair and eat it. I think you'd be less likely to spill." But Corrine continues to eat, standing up.

They Told Children About Things

We saw quality added to interactions when we saw parents telling children more than was necessary in order to answer a question or provide basic education. Parents adapted their utterances, as well as named, repeated, and restated, to help their children understand; they also freely included the children in the adult culture. They read their children material containing vocabulary well beyond the children's comprehension without bothering to simplify or explain the big words. They put words to what their children seemed to be thinking or feeling and passed judgment on the social appropriateness and relative merit of what the children saw and did. They spontaneously elaborated, adding references to places and things their children would not understand for years.

Telling About What Is Worth Noticing and Remembering

This parent is telling her child about an experience and modeling for the child what was worth noticing, naming, and remembering. Note how the parent begins with a high-level general prompt (one she will ask in future years) and works down, making her questions more specific, easier for the child to answer with his limited vocabulary, and finally just tells him the answer.

> The mother initiates, asking Calvin (24 months), "What did we do on Halloween? What did you put on your head and on your body? What did you look like?" When Calvin does not answer, she tells him, "You were a kitty cat." Calvin says, "Wanna get. Where go?" His mother says, "What are you looking for? I know what you're looking for. What used to be on the door handle?"

Calvin says, "Where?" His mother says, "The trick-or-treat bag. We ate up all the candy already." Calvin says, "Where the candy go?" His mother says, "It's all gone in your tummy." Calvin says, "Want some."

Calvin's mother continues, "You dressed up like a kitty cat." Calvin says, "A kitty cat," and his mother asks, "And what did you put on your face?" Calvin says, "Makeup." His mother repeats, "Makeup. You had a black nose and pink cheeks and then we put a pink outfit on you and ears and a tail and you went over to grandpa's and said, 'Trick-or-treat.' Who else did we see on Halloween?" Calvin says, "Ah," and his mother says, "Your dad. Daddy was in Omaha for 2 days." Calvin does not answer.

Telling About What to Expect and How to Cope

The parent is continuously informing the child about every step and all the varied aspects of an activity. Note that the parent provides toys and soap bubbles in an attempt to occupy and distract the child. The parent warns the child of what is to come; then she pauses in preparation and plays for a moment to establish positive affect, warmth, and caring through much naming and describing. Then she warns the child again to "brace himself." As she performs a routine they both hate (washing his hair) she uses talking to maintain, for them both, the positive affect that incidentally makes the words salient.

His mother is giving Mont (22 months) a bath. After saying, "I have to wash your hair in a minute. You don't like it," she bathes him and then initiates, "Turtle," makes motor noises and adds, "Here comes the boat." She repeats and adds, "It's gonna get the turtle." She makes motor noises and says, "Can he go fast? Watch the boat go fast. Goes rrr." Mont imitates, "Rrr," and his mother copies, "Rrr," and says, "The boat goes fast in the water." Mont takes the boat saying, "I get it. There my boat," and babbles something, putting the boat to his mouth. Mont's mother says, "Oh do you drink with the boat?" She suggests, "There's boats on your cup."

Mont says, "That bubble." His mother says, "Are there bubbles on it?" Mont says something incomprehensible and his mother answers, "Yeah, is that hot water?" Mont gasps and his mother says, "Yeah, I thought it would be hot." Mont says, "Hot water." His mother says, "Uh-huh, we're gonna wash your hair." Mont says, "Bubbles." His mother says, "Put bubbles in your hair. All over. Let's see. Maybe we can do it with you sitting up this time. Maybe this'll work better. Every time I lay you down you cry." Mont says, "Ah." His mother says, "Well let's see if we can get it wet like this," and pours a cup of water over Mont's head.

Mont fusses, and his mother says, "Let's just try it and see if I can do it. I don't know if I can or not. Maybe it'll keep you from crying so much." Mont fusses and his mother says, "I know it. You don't like to have your hair washed, do you?" as she soaps his hair. Mont begins to cry and she asks, "What's the matter?" Mont continues to cry, whimpering, "Mommy." As she washes his hair, his mother says, "Now you have bubbles in your hair. Feel them? You can reach up and touch them. Look. That's in your hair. Those bubbles are. I know you hate to have your hair washed. I've never seen anybody who hates it more. Don't you want bubbles in your hair? No? Should I just wash it and get it over with? All right, let's just get it over with. Lean back. Oh, you hate it, don't you?" Mont continues to cry until his mother finishes rinsing his hair.

They Passed Their Interactional Style On to the Next Generation

We do not intend to discuss children's interactions with their siblings (which were relatively few until the children were 2 years old), but we conclude with an example of an exchange that illustrates a sibling behaving like a parent. Note how informative the sister is, how she lets the child choose the label for the picture, and how nice she tries to be even when the child insists on choosing incorrectly.

> Charlene (24 months) is sitting with her mother and her 4-year-old sister Eileen looking at a picture book.
>
> Their mother points, saying, "Oh, what's that little girl doing?" Charlene says, "Little girl," and Eileen answers, "She's messing up." Her mother offers a more precise description, "She's got paint everyplace. Look there on her dress." Eileen elaborates, "And on her panties and on her legs and on her socks," and her mother adds, "On the floor." Charlene says, "Uh-huh," and her mother asks, "What do you. . . . What's their mom saying about that?" Eileen answers, "You're punished." Charlene repeats, "Punished." Her mother corrects, "She's saying, 'Clean up this mess.' "
>
> After reading through the book once, her mother turns it over to Eileen to read and returns to finish washing up in the kitchen. Eileen points to a picture and asks Charlene, "What's that? What do you think he's doing?" Charlene says, "Oh, eat bowl. That bowl." Eileen says, "Oh, eating that bowl. That's ick." Charlene says, "That's ick." Eileen says, "I wouldn't eat dishes if I were him. If my name was Cookie Monster I would eat a whole bunch of sweets." Charlene says, "Yeah, good. Good." Eileen says, "They're not good for you though." Charlene says, "Yeah."
>
> Eileen points to a picture and asks, "Is that a cow?" Charlene says, "No." Eileen corrects her, "Yeah, it's a cow all right. Why do you say it's not a cow?" Charlene says, "Cookie Monster," and Eileen says, "Oh." She points to the letter "c" at the top of the page and says, "Kuh, kuh, kuh. You think that's a cow?" Charlene says, "No." Eileen says, "It is a cow." Charlene says, "It Cookie Monster." Eileen turns the page, points and says, "This is a horse."

We saw that even socializing with a 4-year-old provided quality experience to a child; no special training or
advanced education was necessary, only an adult model
and the child's own experience with the interactional
style transmitted across generations.

Conclusion: Parenting Styles

The examples in this chapter show that we saw
quality interactions in families in which the parents had
all the advantages of higher education, challenging jobs,
substantial incomes, and broad experience; we found
quality interactions in middle- and low-income families
and in families on welfare limited in both present advantages and future prospects for their children. We saw that
quality experience does not depend on parents' material
or educational advantages.

We saw all the parents add quality to interactions
sometimes; none did so all the time. In every family,
many interactions concerned solely the business of getting things and putting them somewhere else. Some
families added quality to interactions more often than
others and displayed more of some of the behaviors than
others. The parenting styles we observed were remarkably consistent individual blends of more or less quality
added more or less often to interactions. We saw the individual styles that different personalities and family
histories made comfortable for parents; we saw children
adapting to and learning from every style.

Quality interactions seemed to come so naturally to
the parents in well-functioning families as to suggest
that a certain amount of quality interaction may be essential to basic language competence. Natural, too,
seemed to be how actively the children evoked quality

interactions. Returning a child's adoring gaze, few parents could resist saying something; seeing a child pause in wonder led parents to name or explain. Fretful children led parents to offer choices. The long-awaited first words of their children drew parents' intense interest and unqualified approval.

All the children had experience with quality interactions, but some children clearly had much more experience than others. Differences in how often quality interactions occurred and the individual blends of the five behaviors in a parent's typical style could be interpreted as indicating the quality of the home environment as a whole. But most of very young children's lives are filled with nurture, and caring is expressed in many different ways. We could not get the observers to agree that they had noticed differences in the quality of the environments they had observed unless we made it clear that we were referring to the quality of the environment of language and interaction. Because it was differences in language and interaction that we had proposed were related to differences in vocabulary growth rates, we set out to quantify the specific features that added quality to language and interaction.

Endnote

1. For details concerning the measures, procedures, and results of this work, see Hart and Risley (1992).

CHAPTER FIVE

Quality Features of Language and Interaction

❖ ❖ ❖ ❖

W e found many examples in the data that typified the quality interactions we saw in everyday parenting. We saw that all the parents sometimes added quality to interactions as they socialized with their children during their daily activities. All the children had experience with quality interactions; the differences between children's experience lay in how often such interactions occurred and in the ways the behaviors that added quality to interactions were blended in a characteristic parenting style.

To examine the differences between children's experience, we needed to quantify the features of the parent behaviors that were adding quality to the interactions we observed. Not all talk is equally informative, and not all parent–child interactions are equally encouraging. Some experiences are of higher quality in their effects on children's learning, and differing amounts and combinations of experience may have differing effects. Our ultimate goal was to quantify categories of significant family experience (see Chapter 7) so that we could examine whether the amount of such experience was more or less related (or unrelated) to the startlingly large differences we discovered both in amount of parent–child interaction across families and in rates of vocabulary growth across children.

The first step in quantification took us to the units of language and interaction we had coded in the database, as described in Chapter 2. We had coded in the data features of language and interaction that, on the basis of our and others' research, we were certain were important to measure. We had coded words by part of speech; we had coded sentences for number of clauses and verb tenses; and we had coded utterances for discourse function, adjacency condition, and valence. The features we had coded in the data corresponded to, and informed, our impressions of what was happening in the families we observed. Therefore, we organize our discussion of the quality features of language and interaction in terms of the sets of variables we coded in the data, noting the links to our impressions.

We describe five sets of variables: two related to the language children hear and three related to the interactions in which they participate. The first set of variables is vocabulary: the words of all kinds that parents use when they just talk. The second set of variables is sentences: the connections between objects and events that parents make when they tell children about things. The third set is discourse functions: the kinds of utterances parents use to prompt children by giving children choices or directives. The fourth set is adjacency conditions: the relation between parent and child behavior when parents listen to their children or initiate to them.

The fifth set of variables is valence: the emotional tone given to interactions in which parents try to be nice or not.

Quality Features of Language

Two interrelated features give quality to the language of everyday parenting. First, the vocabulary parents use as they care for their children acquaints them with all the distinctions the culture makes with different words arranged in different ways. Second, the sentences parents use expose children to the temporal, causal, and qualitative relations that are important to notice, recall, and express in words.

Children's early experience with words accumulates as a dictionary of meanings, synonyms, antonyms, and slang expressions to which later experiences add new entries or refine or elaborate old entries.[1] New experiences are noticed and categorized because they evoke associations with remembered experiences and symbols. Children encouraged to work with language may seek new experiences or practice using words in order to qualify or clarify concepts and make more precise the meanings of existing dictionary entries. They may feel a need to find words for what they see and feel and to store the unfamiliar words they hear. Children's early interactions set up an entire general approach to words as symbols for experience.

Vocabulary

When parents just talk to create or maintain social closeness with their children, letting immediate circumstances determine the words they use, they expose their children to a steady stream of diverse words and expressions associated with all the varied objects the parents and children handle in the varied places they interact. Children hear vocabulary used in connection with many slightly different uses of objects and in relation to many other different words in a variety of sentence structures.

Such parent talk in association with ongoing experience serves to define and label that experience into the referents of the parent's culture. The more often a child hears different words, the more varied are the associated experiences and the more the meanings of the words for the child come to match the range and nuances of the meanings of the words for the speaker and the culture.[2] Even within the consistent routines that establish associations between words and events for infants there is continual variation. For example, as parents dress their children they casually inform them of the range of meaning of the word "clothes." Clothes will be pants and sweater one day and shorts and shirt another, all of which themselves vary in association with words describing color, size, and weight.

When parents talk spontaneously to their children about what they are doing at the moment, the words they use vary with the subtle demands of the circumstances of speaking. The different words they use reflect the variety of experiences they provide their children and the aspects of those experiences they consider important for the children to notice, name, and remember. The invisible curriculum of child rearing focuses parent talk on what children need to know: first the basics, the names of all the things and actions required in order to give and follow directions; then social routines for polite giving and getting; and, finally, preparation for school by naming colors, counting, and reciting name and age.

The vocabulary of basic names and categories parents use when talking to young children lays the foundations for the complex concepts and relationships the children will be asked to understand later on. The diversity of the vocabulary parents use reflects the scope of the knowledge base the parents are putting in place. A propensity to name and describe embraces the visible, external world as well as the inner world of ideas and motivations. In the intimacy of caring for their infants, parents establish much of what their children will know and feel about private and personal things. As they interpret their infants' behaviors, they label and categorize states and actions and legitimatize with words nuances of feeling and attitudes toward one's own body and self.

We had coded the quality features of vocabulary in the data variables assigned to all words and to the different words the parent said to the child. We assigned each word in the data a code for part of speech and speaker. Words were coded as nouns, verbs, modifiers, or functors; parent words were separately coded for whether they were addressed to the child or to other people. (See Chapter 6, endnote 4, for definitions.) The computer program looked up each word in the individual dictionary of the speaker, added the word if it was not listed there, and counted by part of speech each word and each different word (type) used by the speaker in that observation. This process revealed how different the parents were in the number of total words and of different words, especially different nouns and modifiers (adjectives and adverbs), they typically addressed to their children per hour. Some children learning words had much more experience than others hearing objects, actions, and attributes named in the varying contexts of daily life.

Sentences

In choosing what to tell their children about, parents casually transmit the cultural values and expectations embedded in the sentences they use. Parents tell young children about the importance of cleanliness and property rights when they point out, "That's dirty. Put it down," and, "It's his so you need to give it back to him." They describe what is important to remember about past events, "Your grandma gave you that," and what to expect in the future, "You'll break that if you're not careful." They tell children how to think about causes and effects: "Look. The little girl poured some milk and she dumped it on the floor. Do you think she's gonna get a spanking? No, it was an accident, wasn't it?"

Parent talk defines and labels what children should notice and think about the world, their family, and themselves and suggests how interesting and important various objects, events, and relationships are. Words and sentences, internalized as symbols,[3] become a means for organizing experience and rationalizing and relating it, as well as the basis for logical thinking, problem solving, and self-control. The words and expressions that give nuance and preciseness to talk (and, eventually, writing) to other people also serve when talking to oneself as thinking.

We had coded the quality features of sentences in the data variables assigned to clauses and verb tenses. We assigned each sentence a code for the tense of the main verb (present, past, future) and the number of clauses it contained (one to four or more). (See Chapter 6, endnote 4, for definitions.) The computer program counted in each observation the number of sentences containing two or more clauses and the number of past, present, and future tenses the parent used in speaking to the child. This process revealed how different the parents were in the number of connections they typically brought to their children's attention. In some families, an early focus on the names of animals, clothes, and body parts seemed almost deliberately designed to prepare children to use labels to aid recall and organize thinking once the lessons began to focus on culturally important relations concerning property ("Whose is that?"), kinship ("Who is coming to visit?"), history ("What happened?"), and tradition ("What day is it tomorrow?").

Language and Interaction

Interaction is not essential to language learning. Children learn words from television; the alphabet song is a prime example.[4] They learn words from conversations between adults; parents almost never say swear words to their children. But when we see children picking up words from television and other people's conversations, we see how powerful is the influence of affect. Children's television, like the behavior parents display to infants, captures children's attention by associating words with actions, visual contrast, music, routines, and repetition. Words are associated with warmth, enthusiasm, and enjoyment. Parent talk provides opportunities for observational learning about words and sounds; parent affect makes human sounds distinctive, worth listening to, and pleasant to remember.

Children's experiences with language cannot be separated from their experiences with interaction because parent–child talk is saturated with affect. Parents rarely engage toddlers in polite conversation. More often, they instruct, enthuse, yell, or cajole. Children capture equally the emotional tone and the sound patterns of the words they hear. Long before they begin using words, they begin learning about how families interact in the culture,

Hart and Risley

what people are like, and who and how valued the children themselves are. These learnings permeate the language system itself and influence children's motivation to learn and use words.

Quality Features of Interaction

Three interrelated features add quality to interactions: discourse function (the kinds of utterances used), adjacency condition (the relation between the utterances of speaker and listener), and valence (emotional tone).[5]

Children's early experience with interaction, like their experience with language, accumulates as both net and proportional amounts of experience. Net amounts describe experience in terms of the number of words or the number of discourse functions (kinds of utterances) a child hears. Proportional amounts describe experience independent of how many words or discourse functions are heard. Proportional experience with nouns, for example, is expressed as a type/token ratio, the proportion of different nouns among all nouns heard, whether many or few. Proportional experience with questions, for example, describes the proportion of questions among all the kinds of utterances (discourse functions) heard, whether utterances are many or few.

Differing amounts of interaction provide children differing net amounts of experience with the ways utterances are used to produce particular effects and with how turns are taken during conversation. From proportional amounts of experience, children learn about parenting styles. Of all the discourse functions that utterances can encode, for example, parent demands may constitute a larger proportion than parent questions, and thus the parenting style may be described as authoritarian and demanding obedience, rather than authoritative and providing the child choices. Of all the adjacency conditions that interaction entails, for example, parent initiations may constitute a larger proportion than parent responses, and thus the parenting style may be described as controlling the topics of conversation rather than waiting for the child to bring up a topic of interest to the child. Of all the valence, or the affective value, conveyed in parent utterances, affirmatives, for example, may constitute a larger proportion than prohibitions so that the parenting style may be described as approving rather than disapproving.

A parent's typical interaction style cannot be judged on the basis of isolated instances; what a parent says in any immediate context is governed by what the child is doing and by the parent's developmental expectations. We saw parents deal with nagging and attention-getting behavior by ignoring children's initiations; they demanded obedience after gentle guidance had failed. All provided both affirmative and corrective feedback to help their children learn right from wrong. Children adapt to, and learn from, their parents' typical interaction styles; part of what they learn concerns whether parents are often, or seldom, responsive, relatively helpful or highly demanding, mostly approving or frequently negative.

Discourse Functions

Discourse functions categorize utterances in terms of the responses they prompt. Statements assert without requiring a response ("I want you to get your coat on."). Demands prompt action ("Get your coat on."). Questions ask for answers ("Do you have your coat on?"). When parents give choices to very young children, they provide them experience with all these discourse functions because the parents are not yet actually allowing the children to choose, they are teaching them to choose.

In order to teach children to make choices, parents employ three levels of prompts.[6] A parent prompts first with a statement of a social or a family rule. The parent hopes that eventually mere reference to the rule or its reason will suffice as a directive. For example, a parent begins by informing the child, "It's cold. You need to put on a coat before you go outside." If the child does not comply, the parent drops back to the second level of prompting, a question, "Can you get your coat?" If there is still no compliance, perhaps despite persuasion and offers to help, the parent drops back to the third level of prompting, a demand, "Go get your coat," often plus, "now."

Parents prompt more mature language in the same way. As they point, they model by stating, "That's a horse," and pause for the child to imitate both the point and the word. If the child does not respond, they ask, "Can you say 'horse'?" If still no imitation is forthcoming, they drop back to demanding, "Say 'horse'." They teach social routines this way. We heard parents first say, "Thank you," after a child took a proffered cookie; then they began saying, "What do you say?" after giving the child a cookie, followed by, "Say 'thank you'," if the child did not respond appropriately. We saw parents eventually get rid of imitation in the same way; they began asking, "What are you, a mockingbird?" followed if necessary by, "Don't be a copycat."

Parents who prompt their children to choose to say "Thank you," or to imitate an adult model, are teaching their children to take responsibility for social behaviors the parents may actually consider trivial. (Most of the children we observed said "Thank you" more often than their parents did.) They use such questions to encourage children to evaluate their own behavior and to choose to do or say something more mature, more appropriate, or more helpful. Questions beginning "Can you . . . ?" suggest parental confidence that small children are willing but have either forgotten or are not yet skilled or mature enough to do "better." They prepare children for the important questions to come: "Did you remember to . . . ?" or "Was that a nice/fair/smart thing to do?"

We had coded the quality features of discourse functions in the data variables assigned to each parent sentence. Sentences were coded as declaratives (statements), imperatives (demands), or interrogatives (wh-questions, yes/no questions, auxiliary-fronted yes/no questions, and other). (See Chapter 6, endnote 4, for definitions.) The computer program counted in each observation the total number of each variable the parent addressed to the child. This process revealed consistent differences in how parents typically prompted their children. Some parents seemed to begin at the third level and prompt with a directive most of the time; they asked questions to prompt language and information but simply told the child what to do otherwise. Other parents regularly gave their children the experience that statements and questions can both suggest more appropriate behavior and be as imperative as a demand.

Adjacency Conditions

Adjacency conditions categorize the sequence of utterances in an interaction. An utterance that begins an interaction is categorized as an initiation. Subsequent utterances are categorized by their relation to the prior utterance: A subsequent utterance is categorized as a response if a different speaker takes a turn; if the current speaker continues to talk, the utterance is categorized as floorholding. When parents listen, they provide their children experience with these adjacency conditions, which are the ways speakers and listeners cooperate during interaction. One party initiates and the other responds; a speaker can hold the floor for a while but must eventually let the listener take a turn.

When parents listen attentively to what their children have to say, even silence can serve as a response that appreciates the children's practice and participation in language learning. A parent may initiate interaction by watching a child's activity and listening expectantly for the child to comment. Most often, though, parents listen in order to respond. Then they can choose to model language that elaborates a child-chosen topic, they can prompt the child to elaborate or to practice remembered words, or they can correct by rephrasing immature language.[7] For example, a child says, "This soup is good," and the parent models an elaboration, "Yes, it's delicious, isn't it?" A child says, "Cow," and the parent confirms and then holds the floor in order to prompt, "It lives on a farm all right, but look again. Do you remember what that's called? That's a horse. Can you say horse?" A child says, "Her winned," and the parent response models the correct forms, "Well, she almost won, anyway."

Parent responses prompt child responses. Parents make responding easy for children. For example, they ask, "Huh?" so all a child need do is say the same word or words again. They ask yes/no questions, such as "Do you want . . . ?", where a nod is sufficient response. They ask "What?" and "Where?" so a child can just point. Parents encourage responding in order to keep an interaction going and so prepare children for the hard questions to come. A parent asks, "If you get lost and a policeman asks you what your mommy and daddy's names are, what will you say?" The parent's responsiveness and prompts during past interactions assure the child that eventually the parent will make this question simple enough that the child can answer.

Parents hold the floor after responding or initiating in order to explain, amplify, or rephrase their utterances in ways that will help a child understand or that will encourage the child to answer. They also initiate to prompt child responses. Parents sometimes initiate topics so they can test their children's current knowledge and correct and elaborate it through successive prompts and models. But often they initiate just to let children know they are available and interested in hearing a response to "What are you doing?" Or a parent pauses beside a child and describes by way of asking, "Are you feeding your baby?" or "You like those pans, don't you?", modeling what the child might say later on to attract parent conversation about an activity the parent seems to find interesting.

More often, perhaps, parents initiate to change what their children are doing. A parent may be interested in introducing a topic for talk and so initiate, "Look. See the snow coming down?" or, "Listen. Is that Dad's car?" Or a parent may be more interested in compliance than conversation when saying, "Come and eat now," "Put that in the trash for me, would you?" "Be careful with that," or, "We don't throw balls in the house." But parents also initiate to forestall a change in activity; for example, they say, "I'll be right back." And some parents appear to initiate simply to display language as sheer sociability: "April showers bring May flowers. Did you know that?"

Parent initiations that correct what children are doing may have a different effect than corrections made as responses during interactions. When parents initiate to stop or prevent behavior ("Quit that," "Don't touch") there is often an urgency in their voices that, more than the words, communicates danger or displeasure. When parents respond with similar statements ("Quit pulling," "Don't, now") during interactions, the social closeness of shared activity may soften the rebuke for doing something wrong, especially if the parents' next statements prompt something the children can do right.

Parent responses that reflect active listening and sensitivity to children's interests and knowledge, especially parent responses to children's overtures, may be most important to helping children learn words and meanings. But parent initiations may have an even greater impact over the long term. Parents, like children, initiate about what they find interesting and important. The topics parents choose to initiate about reflect the concerns of the culture, the behaviors that are considered appropriate, and the aspects of the environment that are worth noticing and talking about.

We had coded the quality features of adjacency conditions in the data variables assigned to each parent utterance. An utterance was coded as an initiation if 5 seconds or more had elapsed since the parent and child last interacted. An utterance was coded as a response if it was addressed to the child within 5 seconds of a behavior the child addressed to another person (the parent or another adult or child). An utterance was coded as floor-holding if it was addressed to the child within 5 seconds of a preceding parent utterance without the child having taken a turn. The computer program counted in each observation the total number of each variable (initiations, responses, floorholding utterances) the parent addressed to the child. This process revealed consistent differences in parents' individual styles of interacting. Some parents tended to wait and respond to the children's choice of words and topics; others did most of the initiating themselves.

Valence

Valence describes the emotional tone, positive or negative, given to interactions. When parents try to be nice, they give positive valence to interactions. They give positive valence to their initiations by providing children choices of engaging activities and opportunities to participate ("help") in the parents' work and then by initiating to volunteer their appreciation while the children are being "good." In this way, parents not only set the prevailing emotional tone of their initiations but also create a reservoir of positive feelings to ease both them and their children over times of anger and frustration.

More often, parents may use their responses as occasions for giving positive valence to interactions. Just turning away instead of saying, "Clumsy," can give positive valence to an interaction that began with the parent cautioning, "Be especially careful not to drop that now." Most parents, though, especially when their children began saying words, gave explicit approval: "That's right, juice." We saw all the parents give positive affect to interactions by repeating what their children said. To children trying out their first words, parent imitation appeared to be truly the highest form of compliment, a signal that the parent was listening and in enthusiastic agreement that the child had said a meaningful word in the adult's language.

Parent repetitions give positive valence to interactions because they simultaneously confirm, model, prompt, and, often, gently correct what their children say.[8] Parents repeat to confirm their interpretation of an immature pronunciation, for example, "Apple? Is that what you want?" Parent repetitions model the adult version of their children's language so that the children can make an immediate comparison and judge their progress for themselves. Parent imitation prompts child imitation and leads to games devoted to mutual repetition in which parents demonstrate how easily words are learned by copying what other people say. Parent expansions gently correct children. For example, a child says, "What that?", and the parent responds, "Yeah, what is that?" Extensions casually suggest more mature behavior. For example, a child says, "Car," and the parent models the use of the child's word in a phrase, "Yes, a green car." Even after parents put an end to echoing as socially inappropriate they continue to respond, as adults do, by repeating a topic word so that children continue to experience repetition as confirming a listener's interest.

Most of the affirmative feedback we saw given to children was in the form of repetition; even when parents gave explicit approval, they added repetition. When the child said, "I'm 2 years old now," the parent said, "That's right. You're 2 years old now." We saw parents give explicit approval to children's language by saying, "That's right"; they gave explicit approval to children's motor skills by saying, "That's good." In giving their children affirmative feedback, parents casually emphasized a culturally relevant distinction: Words are approved for correctness, actions are approved for agility.

Explicit disapproval was usually directed at "you," as stated in an evaluation, "You're (being) bad," or implied in a prohibition, "Stop acting so mean." All the parents gave explicit disapproval ("Don't do that") just as they all gave affirmative feedback by repeating their children's words. But we saw some parents put considerable effort into arranging activities so they could avoid telling a child, "Don't grab it away from her," or, "Don't spill it," and state instead what the child should do: "Tell her it's your turn now," or "Only fill it up to the line." We saw some parents deliver disapproval and prohibitions in a tone of voice that seemed to convey affection and an approving sense of "bad."

We coded the quality features of valence in the data variables assigned to prohibitions, approval, and repetitions (including expansions and extensions) said in immediate response to a child utterance. Coded as approval were statements explicitly approving of a child's words or actions as "Right" or "Good," and "I love you." Coded as prohibitions were parent directives that specified, "Don't," "Stop," "Quit," or "Shut up," as well as statements explicitly diasapproving of a child's words or actions as "Wrong," "Bad," or "Stupid" and "I hate you." In each observation, the computer program counted the total numbers of approvals, repetitions, and prohibitions the parent addressed to the child and added approvals and repetitions to produce a total of all affirmatives. This process revealed how different children's everyday lives were in how competent and valuable their parents seemed to consider them.

Quality Experience with Language and Interaction

All the quality features of language and interaction were present in the everyday parenting that all the children experienced but in differing amounts. The amount of experience children got with which quality features varied because all the features combined and changed with the places and purposes of interaction. The different words parents used changed as the agenda advanced from providing names for things to describing past and future events. Parent directives changed in form as children became more receptive to hints. Parent responses changed as children learned more sophisticated language, and the emotional tone of interactions changed as children gained skills for testing their parents' patience.

How the quality features of language and interaction combine and interact over time may be seen in incidental teaching at the zone of proximal development (see this chapter, endnote 3). The zone of proximal development is defined as the difference between what a child can do alone and what the child can do with guidance from a more competent member of the culture. A parent provides enough but not too much help; as the child learns to do more and more, the parent gradually removes the support, but if the child falters, the parent quickly renews support. Teaching in the zone of proximal development is less a matter of providing support than of matching the amount of support to the skill level the child displays.

The incidental teaching of language[9] at the zone of proximal development illustrates how the quality features of language and interaction combine. In incidental teaching, a parent begins by responding to the topic the child has initiated. The parent prompts the child to elaborate, recall, or relate the topic to other words and experiences. The parent chooses the prompt for its appropriateness to the topic, the immediate context, and the child's current skill level. Frequent incidental teaching keeps the parent aware of what the child can do without support, where more practice is needed, and what the child is ready to learn next. The parent provides a fuller prompt if the child has difficulty, or the parent simply tells the child the answer. Incidental teaching ends with confirming feedback in which the parent expresses explicit appreciation of the child's use of language.

Children's experience with frequent but brief and encouraging interactions that involve incidental teaching relative to a child-chosen topic may be contrasted to experience with infrequent and discouraging interactions that involve parent initiations to stop or correct what a child is doing. Infrequent interactions combine with frequent prohibitions to limit a child's opportunities both to learn words and to explore the actions and objects they describe. The exchange of social closeness that motivates extended interactions may gradually be lost in the relationship.[10] Parent and child may talk together chiefly because they need to, and what they need to talk about may require only a limited vocabulary.

We had chosen the quality features of language and interaction that were coded in the longitudinal data on the basis of certain assumptions we shared with most developmental researchers concerning what should happen in the course of children's early experience. More interactions during everyday activities should expose children to a greater number of different words and expressions used to name and describe and to more prompts for practice; more practice should lead to more parent responses and approval. More interactions should lead to more experience with what parents consider important that their children notice and remember. In homes in which children are talked to often and discouraging words are seldom heard, children should accumulate more experience with the quality features of language and interaction. Having quantified these quality features, we could return to the striking differences we saw in how much interaction went on in the families and ask whether what should happen in the course of children's early experience actually does happen.

Endnotes

1. Durkin (1987) presented a view of what happens over the years of parent–child interactions. He reminded us that much of parent–child interaction is likely to be focused on "getting things done," and such interactions may not be reliably structured to foster language acquisition. Parents' immediate purposes influence the forms and functions to which utterances are put, thus determining the features of the database available to the child as learner and mediating how the child comes to understand the social world.

2. Nelson (1986) proposed that children represent their everyday experience in event schemas. The schema is a generalized structure made up of slots or categories of event information such as actors, actions, objects, locations, and social and physical interactions. A particular event schema (e.g., a dressing or bathing routine) specifies which acts and information categories are required and which are optional, but the content of any one slot constrains what can fill the remaining slots. The event representations serve as a basis for abstraction of categories, roles, and event hierarchies and shift with development from immediate perceptions to abstract representational structures.

    For a description of language experience and vocabulary development from this perspective, see Harris (1993).

3. Vygotsky (1978) proposed that children learn primarily through social interaction with more capable members of their culture. Through interaction in the zone of proximal development, children gradually learn to perform more and more complex steps in an activity (e.g., dressing); at the same time children are learning that the activity is made up of steps to be successively attended to and mastered. Eventually children "know" the activity: They can both do it and describe it. The parent is not a

teacher as much as a joint participant in such recurring learning opportunities.

Gleason (1985) discussed how parents socialize children through language and interaction to think and act like members of their own social class or cultural group. Because children are literal minded, a parent's words become the voice of the child's conscience, repeating, "Be nice," "Say 'thank you,' " or "Look both ways before you cross the street."

4. Children do learn from television; see Huston, Wright, Rice, Kerkman, and St. Peters (1990).

Walden (1993) suggested that early affective communication may set the stage for social referencing, which may then become a particularly potent form of learning for a child, who must figure out how to feel and behave relative to the many new events encountered every day. Social referencing occurs when children base their personal interpretations of events, and of the words associated with those events, partly or wholly on how they see or hear their parents reacting.

5. A concise and interesting summary of how parent–child conversations may facilitate language development is found in Snow (1986).

6. Goody (1978) used cross-cultural observations to explore what people do when they ask questions and noted that all questions are about commands as well as about information. American parents, unlike those in other countries, seem to make constant use of training questions in order to give their children practice in supplying answers to questions aimed at eliciting information in a systematic way.

In the same volume, Brown and Levinson (1978) used cross-cultural observations to describe the variety of strategies that language makes available for negotiating social relationships. Every culture, it seems, communicates social distance and respect for status differences through polite forms and indirect requests ("I'd like. . . ."

"Would you get. . . .") as well as social closeness and solidarity through imperatives ("Come eat," "Have some more cake.").

7. The classic study of contingent relations between parent and child utterances is Bloom, Rocissano, and Hood (1976). Although the study focused on changes in the child's utterances, the influence of changes in the child's discourse patterns on the adult's response patterns was also noted.

    Moerk (1992) presented a microanalytic study of response relations between parent–child utterances, the teaching properties of parent models and responses, and the effects on the child's acquisition of language.

8. For discussion of forms of repetition (expansion, extension, and immediate and delayed imitation) and the role of imitation in early learning, see Risley (1977a) and Schumaker and Sherman (1978).

9. The method of incidental teaching is described in Hart and Risley (1975, 1978, 1982). White (1985), in a study of the early experiences of children whose older siblings differed in school success, described a parent–child interaction very like incidental teaching in which a parent paused for a moment to talk with the child whenever the child came and initiated a topic.

10. For a discussion of the development of antisocial behavior from early parent–child interactions, see Patterson, DeBaryshe, and Ramsey (1989).

The Early Experience of 42 Typical American Children

❖ ❖ ❖ ❖

We had coded in the data variables the quality features of language and interaction that we saw all the parents providing their children as they socialized with them. We were ready to ask whether the amount of children's experience with the quality features of language and interaction was related to the startlingly large differences we saw between families in the amount of talking and interaction that typically went on.

We had seen that some parents talked much more than others; they exposed their children to many more words than did parents who talked less. We needed to see whether the greater amount of talking that those parents did actually provided their children more experience with the quality features of language and interaction. Talking a lot may be more repetitive and, as a result, less rich in quality features.[1] Fewer interactions richer in nouns, questions, responses, and approval, for example, may contribute more to children's experience than more frequent interactions less rich in these quality features.

We used SES groups to examine the differences in children's experience because we wanted to contrast the extremes of relative advantage. Also, SES was the family factor most strongly associated with differences in the amount of talking by parents. Then we could ask whether, along with all their other advantages, the children in professional families were getting enriched language or whether those other advantages were instead compensating for the unbridled verbosity of their parents. We could also follow up on a question still lingering from the interventions of the War on Poverty: whether welfare children were hearing some sort of impoverished language[2] such that intervention would need to provide them experiences with language richer in quality features than the language they heard at home.

Amount and Richness Defined

We went to the data to examine the *amount* and *richness* of the experience that parents were typically providing their children. To measure *amount*, we averaged the number per observation hour of each quality feature. To measure *richness*, we divided the number of each quality feature in each observation by the number of utterances the parent said in that observation and averaged the resulting proportion as richness per utterance. We could then compare the amount per observation hour of a quality feature (e.g., the number of nouns a child heard per hour) with the richness of that feature (e.g., nouns) in the parent's utterances.

The Reality and Consistency of Quality Features

Appendix A makes the data available for readers to analyze and interpret beyond what we set out to do. Appendix A lists for each family the 13- to 36-month average of each of the quality features of language and interaction we examined. The interrater reliability of each feature is described below.[3] We operationally defined each feature;[4] the interrater reliability assessments assured us that the observers and coders were applying the definitions consistently and appropriately during transcription and coding. We checked that the tapes recorded in the homes were fully transcribed by having a randomly selected portion of 56% of the tapes independently transcribed. We checked whether an independent listener agreed with every word, utterance, and turn during the full hour for 168 transcriptions, 4 from each family. We checked the accuracy of the coding by having the coders independently recode 22 randomly chosen data files. In all the reliability assessments, we checked that the ranges in interrater percentages of agreement did not distinguish particular families and that each observer was equally reliable across families and SES groups.

Our regular reliability checks assured us that the differences we saw between families were real. All the average percentages of interrater agreement shown in Appendix A are above .80. Average percentages of agreement differed for certain quality features, however. We could attribute the perfect agreement on different words, for example, to the elegance of the computer programs that verified the accuracy of the coding. Differences in percentages of agreement on the data from individual families seemed related to the acoustic qualities of the homes, but in none of the reliability checks did we see any consistent differences in percentages of interrater agreement associated with individual observers, SES, or the amount of talking that was transcribed.

For each quality feature listed in Appendix A, we split the data from each family into halves. We counted the number of each quality feature in one half of the observations (even-numbered months) and then verified that the number did not differ appreciably in the other half (odd-numbered months).[5] The split-half reliability for each quality feature we examined is shown in Appendix A. We split each half once more so we could compare the first 6 even-numbered months with the last 6 even-numbered months, for example. Correlations between data halves that continued to be .90 and above assured us that the differences we saw in the numbers of quality features reflected characteristics of families that were durable over the years of observation and the increasing age and skills of the children.

We saw decrements in the correlations between split halves of the data for quality features of parent language that changed as the children learned to talk. Questions and past and future verb tenses (see Appendix A) became proportionately more frequent in parent speech after the children began to talk; the correlations between the first 6 observation months and the last 6 fell below .80. But the overall ranking of the families by SES remained unchanged. In our earlier examinations (see Chapter 3) we had seen consistency in the amount of time families typically spent talking and interacting with their children. We saw the same consistency in the amount of the quality features they addressed to their children. Despite the variability that led to considerable overlap between SES groups, we were confident that the data were showing us characteristic, stable differences between families.

Amount and Richness: Differences with SES

We had seen how different the families were in the amount of talking they did, and we had seen the association between sociability and SES. When we quantified the quality features of language and interaction in the parents' talk to their 1- and 2-year-old children, we again saw major differences between the families associated with SES (see Appendix A; Figures 8–10). We saw that in an average hour the professional parents displayed to their children more words and more different words of all kinds, more multiclause sentences, more past and fu-

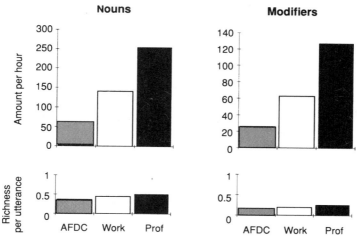

Figure 8.   The amount of parent talk was the major difference between children's early experience with nouns and modifiers. AFDC = 6 welfare families; Work = 23 working-class families; Prof = 13 professional families. (See Appendix B for a detailed explanation of this figure.)

ture verb tenses, more declaratives, and more questions of all kinds. The professional parents also gave their children more affirmative feedback and responded to them more often each hour they were together.

The utterances of the professional parents were not only greater in amount but also richer in certain quality features. Nouns, modifiers, past-tense verbs, auxiliary-fronted yes/no questions, declarative sentences, and affirmative feedback occurred proportionately more often in the utterances of the professional parents. Despite interacting more often with their children, though, the professional parents displayed no more imperatives per hour; they initiated interaction with their children no more often per hour, and they displayed less negative feedback to their children per hour, than the other parents.

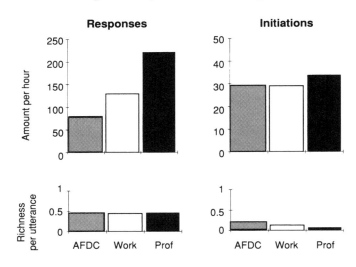

Figure 9.   Parents who talked more responded more, but did not initiate more. AFDC = 6 welfare families; Work = 23 working-class families; Prof = 13 professional families. (See Appendix B for a detailed explanation of this figure.)

124

In the welfare families, the utterances addressed to the children were both fewer in quantity and somewhat less rich in nouns, modifiers, verbs, past-tense verbs, and clauses. Although the welfare parents were just as likely to respond to their children and ask them questions, they displayed fewer floorholding utterances—after initiating or responding, these parents continued talking to their children less than half as often as did the working-class parents. The result was that the welfare children received in each hour of their lives less than half the language experience of the working-class children.

A major difference associated with social strata was in the amounts of prohibition parents gave their children. The professional parents gave their children an average of 5 prohibitions per hour; the welfare parents gave

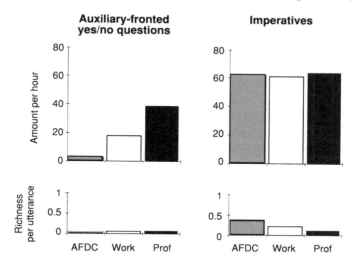

Figure 10. Parents who talked more asked more questions, but did not make more demands. AFDC = 6 welfare families; Work = 23 working-class families; Prof = 13 professional families. (See Appendix B for a detailed explanation of this figure.)

their children an average of 11. But the difference in amounts of talk was such that the relative richness of prohibitions in the utterances of the welfare families was 7 times the richness of prohibitions in the utterances of the professional families. Similarly, though the welfare parents initiated interaction with their children no less often than the professional parents and used imperatives no less often, the lesser amount of talk led to interactions richer in imperatives and initiations and made parent initiations of negative imperatives ("Don't," "Stop," "Quit") a much more prominent part of the welfare children's experience.

There was a striking difference, too, in affirmative feedback. The professional parents gave their children affirmative feedback every other minute, more than 30 times per hour, twice as often as the working-class parents gave their children affirmative feedback and more than 5 times as often as parents in welfare families gave their children affirmative feedback. The children in welfare families heard a prohibition twice as often as they heard affirmative feedback.

Amount and Richness: Differences in Children's Experience

We used regression analysis[6] to examine the relative contributions of amount and richness to how much experience children got per hour with each quality feature of parent language and interaction. The partial correlations shown in Appendix A indicate the relationship between how much of each quality feature a child heard and its amount and richness in parent speech when each variable (amount, richness) was separated from the effects of the other variable. For example, the number of nouns a child heard was more strongly related (partial $r = .98$) to the amount of utterances a parent addressed to the child and less strongly related (partial $r = .88$) to the richness of nouns in the parent's utterances.

Across almost all the quality features, the amount of talking was contributing more to the number of quality features children experienced in an hour of family life than was the richness of those quality features in parent utterances. Even the highly educated parents gave their children more experience with the quality features of language through the extraordinary amount of their talk rather than through the relative richness of quality features in their utterances. Children in welfare families received less than half the language experience of working-class children in each hour of their lives, due more to the lesser amount of talking in the family than because their parents' utterances were somewhat less rich in quality features.

Our surprise that the amount of parent language seemed to be contributing as much to children's experience as the richness of quality features in parent utterances led us to look at whether individual parents actually gave their children more experience with the quality features of language when the parents talked more to the children. We compared for each family the averages from the three observations in which the parent talked least to the child with the averages from the three observations in which the parent talked most to the child [7] (see Figures 11 and 12).

From these comparisons we saw that the richness of quality features in parent utterances hardly varied. Whether a parent talked a lot or a little, such quality features as different words, questions, clauses, past-tense verbs, and affirmatives and prohibitions occurred ap-

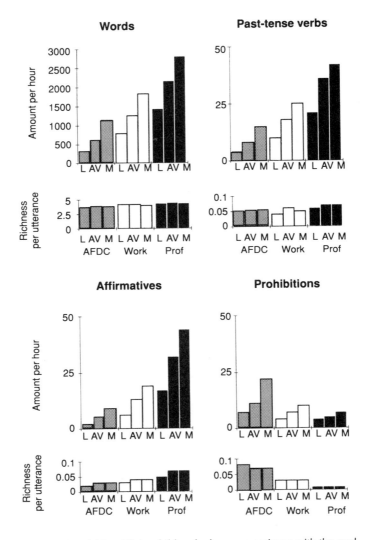

Words

Past-tense verbs

Affirmatives

Prohibitions

Figures 11 and 12.   All the children had more experience with the quality features of language and interaction when their parents talked more (M) than average (AV) and less when their parents talked least (L). (See Appendix B for a detailed explanation of these figures.)

proximately equally often per parent utterance. In those observations in which the parents averaged almost 500 utterances per hour, the mean number of words was 4.0 per utterance; it was 4.1 per utterance when they averaged fewer than 250 utterances per hour. Questions per utterance was .24 when parents averaged almost 500 utterances and .26 when they averaged fewer than 250.

The amount of the quality features a child heard differed greatly, however. Because the richness of quality features in parent utterances did not vary, an average of almost 500 parent utterances per hour exposed a child to an average of 124 questions, 25 affirmatives, and 341 different words in an hour. An average of fewer than 250 utterances per hour exposed the child to an average of 59 questions, 9 affirmatives, and 208 different words in an hour.

We saw within families the differences in the child's experience when the amount of parent talk varied. In the 3 hours she talked most to her child, one parent said an average of 725 utterances, with 4.4 words per utterance. The richness of questions was .29; of affirmatives, .05; and of prohibitions, .02. The child heard 459 different words, 210 questions, 30 affirmatives, and 13 prohibitions. In the 3 hours this parent talked least to her child, she said an average of 470 utterances, with 4.2 words per utterance. The richness of questions was .31; of affirmatives, .05; and of prohibitions, .02. The child heard 363 different words, 147 questions, 24 affirmatives, and 8 prohibitions. Because the richness of these quality features in the parent's utterances varied so little, the child gained more experience with the quality features of language and interaction at those times the parent talked more.

We saw the magnitude of the differences in children's experience when we looked at the range in the amount parents talked to their children. Another parent, in the 3 hours she talked most to her child, said an average of 198 utterances, with 4.0 words per utterance. The richness of questions was .19; of affirmatives, .02; and of prohibitions, .04. The child heard 191 different words, 38 questions, 3 affirmatives, and 7 prohibitions. In the 3 hours this parent talked least to her child, she said an average of 39 utterances, with 4.1 words per utterance. The richness of questions was .18; of affirmatives, .01; and of prohibitions, .04. The child heard 59 different words, 7 questions, 1 affirmative, and 1 prohibition.

Both of these children gained more experience with the quality features of language and interaction in those hours when their parents talked more. Although the utterances of the second parent were somewhat less rich in quality features than those of the first parent, we can speculate about what the second child's experience might have been had the parent ever talked as much to the child as the first parent did when she talked least to her child.

Everyday Parent Talk

When we saw the results of our comparisons we realized why, when we were observing, we had noticed differences in amounts of talking in the families but had not noticed differences in richness. We were transcribing major differences in amounts of talk, but we were listening to all the parents talk with their 1- and 2-year-olds in much the same manner. Rather than any evidence of impoverished language, we saw, relative to talk to adults, a general reduction of richness in utterances addressed to small children. All the parents talked about the here and now, adapting what they said to a child's immature understanding linked to a short attention span. Talking appropriately to children who were just beginning to learn language limited for all the parents alike the topics they could introduce, restricted the complexity of the sentences they could use, and required frequent repetition of the same words across the varying contexts and regular confirmation of children's attempts at words.

When the parents talked more, they did not change their usual style: Their utterances continued to be appropriate and much the same in relative richness. But more talk meant more subtle variations in immediate context, calling for more different words. When parents talked more, they asked more questions, particularly auxiliary-fronted yes/no questions such as, "Can you say hi to Daddy?", to prompt their children to participate, and they held the floor longer to keep interaction going. We saw that talking a lot, rather than diluting richness in the utterances children hear, increases the amount of experience children have with nearly all the quality features of language.

Extrapolating Amounts of Language Experience

The differences in language experience between children in welfare and working-class families and between children in working-class and professional families that were produced by differences in family sociability were consistent across daily variations in family life and persistent throughout the time the children were learning to talk. A simple extrapolation of these differences in hourly experience across the children's waking hours would indicate differences in cumulative experience of enormous magnitude between the children of welfare and working-class families and between the children of working-class and professional families.

To illustrate the differences in the amount of children's language experience using numbers, rather than just "more" and "less," we can derive an estimate based simply on words heard per hour. The longitudinal data showed that in the everyday interactions at home, the average (rounded) number of words children heard per hour was 2,150 in the professional families, 1,250 in the working-class families, and 620 in the welfare families (see Figure 7). Extrapolating these average amounts of language experience (in terms of words heard per hour) to the approximately 100 hours of family life per week (given a 14-hour waking day), the working-class children would have 125,000 words of language experience per week, and the welfare children would have 62,000 words of language experience. This leaves a difference of more than 60,000 words every week between the welfare children and the working-class children when they were 1–2 years old. If we extrapolate these differences to 1 year, the working-class children would have more than 6 million words of language experience; the welfare children would have more than 3 million.

Given the consistency we saw in the data, we might venture to extrapolate to the first 3 years of life. By age 3 the children in professional families would have heard more than 30 million words, the children in working-class families 20 million, and the children in welfare families 10 million. To equalize the cumulative experience of the welfare children at age 3 to that of the working-class children in the number of words said to them would require the addition of 12 million words. That is 1 year's worth of words heard by a child in a professional family, and 1 1/2 years worth of words for a child in a working-class family. And we have not yet considered any of the other quality features of language and interaction or the children's well-established trajectories of vocabulary growth.

Cumulative Experience with Language

The differences we saw between families seemed to reflect the cultural priorities parents casually transmit through talking. In the professional families the extraordinary amount of talk, the many different words, and the greater richness of nouns, modifiers, and past-tense verbs in parent utterances suggested a culture concerned with names, relationships, and recall. Parents seemed to be preparing their children to participate in a culture concerned with symbols and analytic problem solving. To ensure their children access to advanced education, parents spent time and effort developing their children's potential, asking questions and using affirmatives to encourage their children to listen, to notice how words refer and relate, and to practice the distinctions to be made among them. Effort meant attending closely to what their children said and did and adapting talk promptly and adroitly in order to challenge and guide exploration. Especially important was keeping their children engaged with adults and practicing language in the presence of more skilled models of the culture.

In the welfare families, the lesser amount of talk with its more frequent parent-initiated topics, imperatives, and prohibitions suggested a culture concerned with established customs. To teach socially acceptable behavior, language rich in nouns and modifiers was not called for; obedience, politeness, and conformity were more likely to be the keys to survival. Rather than attempting to prepare their children with the knowledge and skills required in a technological world with which the parents had had little experience, parents seemed to be preparing their children realistically for the jobs likely to be open to them, jobs in which success and advancement would be determined by attitude, how well the children presented themselves, and whether they could prove themselves through their performance.

Among the working-class families we saw a mixture of these cultures. We saw upwardly mobile families in which the parents named, prompted, and tested with all the intensity and adaptability of the professional parents and at the same time used imperatives and prohibitions to convey expectations for obedience and conformity similar to those of the welfare parents. We saw one parent take time from a job and a large family to intervene for an intense 3 months of prompting the child to name, relate, recall, and describe. Another parent often used imperatives and prohibitions to demand appropriate behavior: paying attention to the words on *Sesame Street*.

We saw that all the quality features of parent language and interaction were so highly related to one another and so substantial and consistent in their proportions that by the time the children were 3 years old, the cumulative experience their parents had provided them differed enormously in both amount and kind. If these quality features were truly important and if the cumulative differences in the children's experience with them were even approximately as great as our extrapolations suggested, these quality features should be strongly linked to the children's accomplishments at age 3 and later. We would have been amazed, and baffled, had we found otherwise.

Endnotes

1. More talking was not, however, more repetitious in terms of utterances. We assigned a particular code to an utterance if it was a verbatim repeat or a rephrasing of an immediately preceding utterance. A rephrasing was defined as a change in only one contentive word (e.g., "I'm going" followed by "I'm leaving"). An average of 13% of parent utterances were verbatim repeats or rephrasings of an immediately preceding utterance; the range was from 3% to 36%. Of the 20 parents below the average of 341 utterances per hour, 6 were below and 14 were above the average of 13%. None of the parents above average in amount of talk were above the average in repetitions and rephrasings.

2. Bernstein (1970) proposed a theory concerning family transmission of social roles that generated considerable controversy during the War on Poverty by suggesting that lower-class children might have some sort of language deficit. Bernstein described differences in apparent ability to switch grammar and vocabulary according to speech context. The elaborated codes used by upper-class children were said to be more flexible and less context dependent than the restricted codes characteristic of lower-class children's speech.

3. Appendix A shows for each of the 42 families the amount and richness of the quality features of parent language and interaction averaged over the hours of observation during the months the children were 13–36 months old. Families were ranked by the socioeconomic index derived from Stevens and Cho (1985); see Chapter 3, endnote 4. The welfare families were ranked in descending order by parent years of education. For definitions of the variables, see this chapter, endnote 4. It may be seen that parent initiations, responses, and floorholding turns sum approximately to total utterances; the differences are due to rounding the numbers.

The richness per utterance of each quality feature was derived for each individual observation by dividing the amount of the feature by the number of utterances in that observation. The per observation richness was then averaged across the 24 months.

All the analyses were performed by SPSS/PC+™ V2.0 (1988) statistical programs.

The correlation coefficients listed in Appendix A are only those significant at the .001 level. Asterisks indicate relationships with significance levels between .001 and .01. Relationships with significance levels larger than .01 are indicated by ns (not significant).

Interrater percentages of agreement derive from three separate reliability assessments, as follows.

1) Utterances. One of the observers who did not record in the family listened to a tape and independently transcribed a randomly selected portion of approximately 2 minutes (a handwritten page) of the tape. Across the 2 1/2 years of observing, 56% of the tapes were thus independently transcribed. The independent transcription was matched to the original observer's transcription for the number and sequence of utterances, vocal or verbal. Utterances missing, differing in segmentation, or out of sequence were counted as disagreements. Agreements were divided by agreements plus disagreements; average agreement was .95 (range .79–1.00 per family).

2) Words, initiations, responses, and floorholding turns. Randomly selected for each child were four observations, two from the first year of observation when the children were just beginning to say words and two from the second year when the children were talking fluently. Each of the three observers checked one sample from each year from each family in which she was not the observer. The observer listened independently to the tape as she read the

coded original transcript of the tape; she noted agreement or disagreement with each word, segmentation of the utterance, and utterance code (i.e., whether the utterance was an initiation, a response, or a floorholding turn). She added each omitted word as a disagreement. Total agreements that the independent observer reported on each category were then divided by the totals for that category reported in the computer processing of that observation. Average agreement was .99 on the exact words parents said to the child (range .87–1.00 per family) and .99 on the utterance codes (range .97–1.00 per family).

3) Word types (nouns, verbs, modifiers, and functors) and sentence (clauses, past, future) and interaction (declaratives, imperatives, questions, affirmatives, and prohibitions) codes. We independently recoded one randomly selected observation from the final year of observation for 22 families randomly selected from the 42. The recoding replicated the process of the original coding as described in Chapter 2 and benefited from the computer programs that had prompted and verified each step in the original coding of the data. A computer program then matched the original and recoded observations line-by-line and counted the codes that matched. Agreements were divided by agreements plus disagreements; average agreement on word types was 1.00 (range 1.00–1.00) and .84 on sentence and interaction codes (range .60–.95 per family).

In Appendix A, the split-half reliability shows the correlation between the data recorded in the observations from the even- and odd-numbered months; see this chapter, endnote 5.

The partial correlations in Appendix A are the results of a series of regression analyses (see this chapter, endnote 6) in which the dependent variable was the amount per hour of a given quality feature of language or interaction and the independent variables were utterances heard per hour and the richness per utterance of the given quality feature.

Also shown in Appendix A are the correlations between each quality feature and the measures of child accomplishment (vocabulary growth, vocabulary use, Stanford-Binet IQ score) described in Chapter 7.

4. We used textbook definitions for the quality features of vocabulary. We used a standard dictionary to define words as nouns, verbs, modifiers (adjectives and adverbs), and functors (all other words—determiners, articles, quantifiers, pronouns, prepositions, conjunctions). Proper nouns (names, days of the week), animal noises, and coined words (not listed in the standard dictionary) were assigned a separate code and were not included in the count of different words. Different words were identified for each speaker by the computer program that compared each word in an observation to the compiled dictionary for that speaker.

Utterances were segmented on the basis of pause length (allowing for mid-utterance hesitations) and syntactic and prosodic properties. Each utterance was coded for the speaker as an initiation (talk after noninteraction for 5 seconds or more), a response (talk within 5 seconds of another speaker's utterance), or a floorholding turn (talk following within 5 seconds of a prior utterance of the same speaker with no intervening speech by anyone else).

Sentences were coded as present, past, or future on the basis of the tense of the verb in the main clause. Future was coded for "will," "'ll," and "gonna."

Two or more clauses were coded when an utterance contained a noun clause ("I want you to do it"), adverbial clause ("you can have it when/before/after you. . ."), a relative clause ("that's the one I want"), or conjoined sentences ("Go and find it.").

Sentences (utterances containing a verb) were coded as declaratives unless they were imperatives ("You do it," or "Do it") or questions. The observers noted on the transcripts intonational questions (e.g., "Got it?") or declaratives with missing subjects (e.g., "[I] got it.").

Questions were wh-questions (asking "Who," "What," "Where," "When," "Why", or "How"), questions answerable with "Yes" or "No," and other questions (alternatives, e.g., "Is it a cat or a dog?"). A code was added to yes/no questions for auxiliary fronting when a verb appeared before the pronoun ("Do you want it?" rather than "You want it?" or "Want it?").

Affirmatives were explicit parent approval ("That's good/right," "I love you") and utterances immediately following a child utterance that used one or more of the child's contentive words in a repetition, an expansion of the child's utterance into a more acceptable form, or an extension that added words to the child's utterance.

Prohibitions were explicit parent disapproval ("You are/That's bad/wrong," "I hate you") and imperatives specifying, "Don't," "Stop," "Quit," or "Shut up."

5. We used split-half reliability to verify the stability across observations of the amount and richness of each quality feature of parent language and interaction. We divided the data into even-numbered months of child age (8–36 months) and odd-numbered months of child age (7–35 months) and derived the correlation between each feature across the halves. We found we would have obtained almost identical data had we observed only every other month over the 2 years.

6. We used regression analysis despite violating its assumptions because it permits the comparisons we wanted to examine. We knew that in spontaneous speech such quality features as nouns are not normally distributed in an hour of utterances, and because the features we examined were not independent aspects of language, we expected the strong relationships we saw between the amount and richness of each feature. When the richness variables were proportions we used an arc sine transformation. We used

split halves of the data to test the findings from each primary regression analysis. In the output from the analyses we ignored statistical significance and considered only the partial correlations indicating the relationships between how much of a quality feature a child hears and its amount and richness in parent speech when each variable (amount and richness) is separated from the effects of the other variable.

7. After eliminating any less than ordinary observations (e.g., when the parent was reading a book or when more or fewer than the usual number of family members were present), we averaged the observations in which the parent said the fewest and the most utterances per hour in three periods—when the child was 11–18 months old, 19–27 months old, and 28–36 months old—in order to take into account changes in interaction with the increasing maturity of the child.

CHAPTER SEVEN

Accomplishments of the 42 Children at Age 3 and Later

❖ ❖ ❖ ❖

W
hen we quantified the quality features of language and interaction we saw consistent differences in the amount of children's experience with language before they were 3 years old. Some children had heard far more language than others and considerably more of the quality features of the language they would need to master. Some children were encouraged far more often to display what they had learned of the language so far and given vastly more affirmative feedback for doing so.

The children, like their families, were remarkably individual; even as infants they were different in personality traits and preferred activities. At age 3 when we ended observation, these differences led them to talk in differing amounts about different things. But by age 3 they were all using language appropriately. They were using clauses and tenses and a varied vocabulary just as their parents did. Nearly all were talking fluently, most more than their parents talked to them.

The observers saw only how normal all the children were. Differences in intelligence and in the complexity of the language they used were made invisible by how competently all the children solved problems and how flexibly they expressed themselves. At 36 months, a difference between an IQ score of 80 and 120 amounts to only 6 months difference in mental age above and below the average. Only people with special training (usually armed with a standardized test) are likely to distinguish a 6-month difference in mental age within the variability of children's behavior.

We needed to measure the children's status at age 3. We had undertaken the observations to study the association between early experience and later language performance, and we had measured the amount and richness of the children's early experience with language and interaction. Now we needed measures of the children's language performance. We knew that the many differences among the children in activity level, emotionality, and family status would continue to influence how the children performed. We chose to focus on accomplishments at age 3 that were likely to be linked to later language performance in school: vocabulary growth, vocabulary use, and IQ score.

Measures of Accomplishment

Vocabulary Growth

Vocabulary growth reflects a child's rate of language learning in terms of how often the child is adding new words to the vocabulary that make distinctions among old words or that represent new concepts. We measured vocabulary growth as the trajectory of expressive vocabulary change at age 3. David Thissen, a senior statistician, provided us a statistical description of each child's growth curve, which he derived from a multilevel nonlinear analysis of each child's cumulative vocabulary over the years of observation.[1] The final parameter in the multilevel model of the growth curve projected the trajectory of the curve as the logarithm of the number of words acquired in this early period. Vocabulary growth indicates how steadily a child is learning new words for naming and describing things and actions and their relations.

Vocabulary Use

Vocabulary use reflects a child's cognitive functioning in daily interaction with experience and predicts the complexity of other people's responses to the child.[2] We measured vocabulary use as the number of different words a child used per hour averaged at 34–36 months of age. The number of different words a child uses indicates simultaneously how much the child is talking, how varied are the topics and contexts of talk, and the size of the vocabulary from which the child can draw. The more sophisticated the ideas the child tries to express, the more the child has probably learned in the past and the more the child needs to call past learnings into present conversation. Vocabulary use indicates how many different things, actions, and relations a child talks about from day to day.

IQ Test Score

We consider an IQ score at age 3 to provide a valid estimate of the amount a child has learned in 36 months of life rather than an estimate of the child's capacities.[3] The Stanford-Binet Intelligence Scale was given to each child at age 3 within a month after the conclusion of observations. A professional psychologist not associated with the longitudinal study administered the test. The IQ score indicates how well a child can understand and perform relative to other children of the same age all the various tasks in the Stanford-Binet IQ test.

All the measures of accomplishment at age 3 were highly related. Vocabulary growth (rate of learning words representing new concepts and distinctions between words) was strongly associated with vocabulary use (cognitive functioning in interaction with daily experience) ($r = .92$). Both rate of vocabulary growth and vocabulary use were strongly associated with general accomplishment as estimated by IQ score ($rs = .70$ and $.73$). All three measures of accomplishment at age 3 were strongly associated with family SES. The measures specific to language—vocabulary growth and vocabulary use—were most strongly associated with SES ($rs = .65$ and $.63$); IQ (general accomplishment) was somewhat less strongly associated with SES ($r = .54$).

The Strength of Relationships Between Experience and Accomplishments

We were surprised to see just how strongly the differences in the children's experience were related to differences in their accomplishments. Appendix A shows the correlation between each quality feature and each measure of child accomplishment. Some of the quality features could account for half of the differences in children's accomplishments ($r = .71$, r square $= .50$); such relationships might turn up by chance less than once in every 10,000 calculations involving 42 children ($p < .0001$). The extreme effort and care taken in collecting the data, the large amount of data on each child, and the considerable number and variety of families observed had rewarded us by revealing robust relationships between children's early experience at home and their later accomplishments.

With data this rich in relationships we could afford to be profligate: We note and discuss only features of the children's experience that accounted for more than a quarter of the variance in the children's accomplishments ($r = .50$, $p < .001$). We show the data in Appendix A to invite others to analyze and interpret beyond what we have done here. For the sake of convention, we have marked lesser relationships whose chance occurrence would be less than 1 in 100, but we have considered nonsignificant any relationships in the $p < .05$ and $p > .01$ range most familiar in social science publications.

Child Accomplishments and Quality Features of Language and Interaction

We saw that when parents talked more, their children got more experience with nearly all the quality features of language and interaction and that more talk did not dilute the richness of quality features in the utterances children heard. We saw robust relationships between three quarters of all the quality features we had measured and one or more of the children's accomplishments at age 3. We needed to identify which were the most important quality features of children's early experience with language and interaction. To do so we compared individual quality features of language and interaction with one another to see which were more strongly related to the children's accomplishments at age 3.

Compared with general parent talkativeness, measured as utterances of all kinds said to a child per hour, the number of words a parent said per hour was more strongly related to the child's rate of vocabulary growth, vocabulary use at age 3, and general accomplishments measured in IQ score.

Compared with the number of words the parent said per hour, the number of nouns, verbs, modifiers, and functors the parent said per hour was equally strongly related to child accomplishments, but the number of different words of all types the parent said per hour was more strongly related to all of the child's accomplishments at age 3. Compared with the number of words the parent said per hour, the number of sentences the parent said per hour that contained two or more clauses and that were wh-questions or yes/no questions was equally strongly related to child accomplishments, but the number of sentences that contained past-tense verbs or were auxiliary-fronted yes/no questions was more strongly related to all child accomplishments at age 3. All these features of parent language were most strongly related to child vocabulary use and slightly less related to rate of vocabulary growth and general child accomplishments as estimated by Stanford-Binet IQ test score.

We asked whether the richness of some quality features of language and interaction is important over and above the amount of exposure to those features. The richness of words of any kind in parent utterances, of modifiers and functors, of past-tense verbs, of questions of all types, of yes/no questions, auxiliary-fronted yes/no questions, and affirmatives was somewhat more strongly related to rates of vocabulary growth and to children's general accomplishments at age 3 than was the amount of these features the children heard. The richness of nouns and declaratives in parent utterances was more strongly related to rate of vocabulary growth than was the number of nouns and declaratives parents said to their children.

146

We asked whether any features in parent talk were related to child accomplishments in richness but not amount. We found only three quality features of interaction for which amount was not related to the three measures of child accomplishment while richness was related. All the correlations were negative. The net amount of parent initiations, imperatives, and prohibitions a child heard per hour made no difference to the child's accomplishments at age 3, but the richer the parent's utterances to the child were in initiations, imperatives, and prohibitions, the less rapid was the child's vocabulary growth, the less varied was the child's vocabulary use, and the fewer were the child's general accomplishments as estimated by the Stanford-Binet IQ test. We saw the powerful dampening effects on development when relatively more of the child's interactions began with a parent-initiated imperative ("Don't," "Stop," "Quit") that prohibited what the child was doing.

Family SES and Quality
Features of Language and Interaction

Because the correlations between the measures of accomplishment and family SES differed in strength, we asked which quality features were more strongly associated with each measure of accomplishment than with family SES. Vocabulary growth at age 3 was strongly correlated with family SES ($r = .65$). But the richness of modifiers and auxiliary-fronted yes/no questions in parent utterances, higher proportions of affirmatives, and lower proportions of imperatives were each more strongly correlated with vocabulary growth than was family SES.

Vocabulary use (the number of different words children used per hour at age 3) was also strongly correlated with family SES ($r = .63$). As might be expected, the number of different words of all types parents said to their children per hour over the preceding 2 years was much more strongly related to the children's vocabulary use than was their parents' SES. Also more strongly related than family SES to the amount and variety of vocabulary the children were using at age 3 were the absolute number per hour of modifiers, past-tense verbs, and affirmatives the children had heard, the richness of modifiers and past-tense verbs, the scarcity of imperatives, and the lower proportion of initiations in their parents' utterances.

As expected, the children's performance on the variety of tasks contained in the Stanford-Binet IQ test battery, were robustly associated with their family SES ($r =$ .54). But many of the quality features of the language and interaction they had experienced were even more robustly associated with the children's general accomplishments as measured by the IQ test. The richness of nouns, modifiers, and past-tense verbs in their parents' utterances; their parents' high propensity to ask yes/no questions, especially auxiliary-fronted yes/no questions; and their parents' low propensity to initiate and use imperatives and prohibitions were more strongly predictive of the children's performance on the Stanford-Binet IQ test battery than was family SES.

Categories of Significant Family Experience

We examined the quality features of language and interaction individually to see which were more strongly related to children's accomplishments than to their family's social and economic status. Those quality features that were more strongly related to children's accomplishments than were the advantages conferred by SES we then as-

sembled into logical combinations that would characterize categories of significant family experience with language and interaction and correspond to our impressions
of the parent behaviors that added quality to everyday socializing with children (see Table 2). The categories of significant family experience were exemplified in five
derived variables: Language Diversity, Feedback Tone,
Symbolic Emphasis, Guidance Style, and Responsiveness
(see Figures 13–17).

Table 2.   Links between impressions of parent behaviors and quantifications

Impressions of parent behaviors described in examples	Sets of quality features coded in data variables	Categories of significant family experience exemplified in derived variables
They just talked	Vocabulary: all words, all different words (nouns, modifiers, verbs, functors)	Language Diversity: sum of different nouns plus different modifiers used per hour
They tried to be nice	Valence: approvals, repetitions, prohibitions	Feedback Tone: affirmatives (approval plus repetition) divided by affirmatives plus prohibitions per hour
They told children about things	Sentences: clauses, verb tenses (past, present, future)	Symbolic Emphasis: sum of nouns, modifiers, past-tense verbs per hour divided by utterances per hour
They gave children choices	Discourse functions: declaratives, imperatives, interrogatives (wh-questions, yes/no questions, auxiliary-fronted yes/no questions)	Guidance Style: Auxiliary-fronted yes/no questions divided by auxiliary-fronted yes/no questions plus imperatives per hour
They listened	Adjacency conditions: initiations, responses, floorholding	Responsiveness: responses minus initiations divided by responses per hour

Language Diversity

Language Diversity denotes the amount of a child's experience with language. The more often a child hears words used in association with a variety of events and other words, the more varied and refined are the meanings of words for the child. The variety of experiences that a parent talks about to the child is reflected in the number of different words the parent uses. We used the sum of the number of different nouns and different modifiers a parent said per hour to exemplify Language Diversity. These two quality features were more strongly related to all the measures of child accomplishments than was the sum of all different words; these features reflect particularly well the relationship between talking in more varied contexts and naming and describing a greater variety of objects and their attributes.

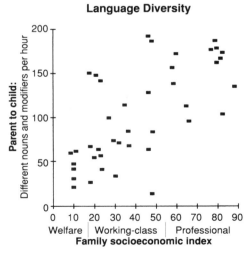

Figure 13. Each square is the characteristic Language Diversity of an individual parent's talk. (See Appendix B for a detailed explanation of this figure.)

Feedback Tone

Feedback Tone denotes the prevailing affect of parent–child interactions. Parent feedback may encourage a child to attend to and participate in language learning or it may discourage the child from working with words. To exemplify Feedback Tone we used the proportion of feedback to the child that was positive. We divided the amount of positive feedback (parent repetitions, extensions, expansions of child utterances, confirmations, praise, approval) per hour by the amount of all feedback, positive plus negative (imperatives to warn or prohibit, disconfirmations, criticisms, disparagements), per hour in order to combine these contrasting characteristics in a single variable descriptive of a child's typical interactions.

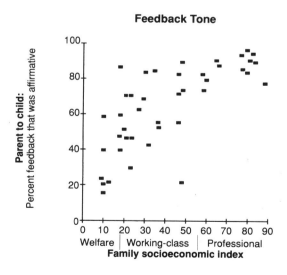

Figure 14. Each square is the Feedback Tone characteristic of an individual parent's interactions. (See Appendix B for a detailed explanation of this figure.)

151

Symbolic Emphasis

Symbolic Emphasis denotes the relative amount of a child's experience with language that refers to relations between things and events. In the aspects of experience parents choose to talk about, they casually emphasize what the culture expects children to notice, name, recall, and relate to other words and experiences in speaking and thinking. To exemplify Symbolic Emphasis we used the richness of nouns, modifiers, and past-tense verbs in parent utterances per hour. We divided the sum of the nouns, modifiers, and past-tense verbs a child heard per hour by the number of utterances the child heard per hour to combine into one variable the three quality features of language individually most strongly associated with child accomplishments at 3.

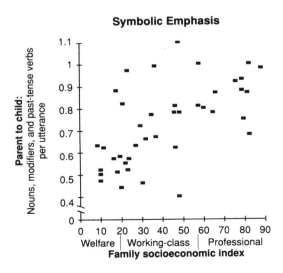

Figure 15.   Each square is the Symbolic Emphasis characteristic of an individual parent's talk. (See Appendix B for a detailed explanation of this figure.)

Guidance Style

Guidance Style denotes the relative amount of prompting a child experiences: how often the child is asked rather than told what to do. Parent prompts suggest a more appropriate behavior, or a more correct label or sentence structure and ask the child to choose the more mature form; such prompts imply the parent's confidence that the child is motivated to improve and does not need to be ordered to do so. To exemplify Guidance Style we used the proportion of guidance that took the form of auxiliary-fronted yes/no questions ("Can you. . ." "Do you. . ." "Shall we. . ." "Is it. . ." "Are they. . ."). We divided the number per hour of auxiliary-fronted yes/no questions by the number of auxiliary-fronted yes/no questions plus the number of imperatives per hour in order to combine these contrasting quality features in a single characteristic descriptive of a child's typical experience in receiving directives.

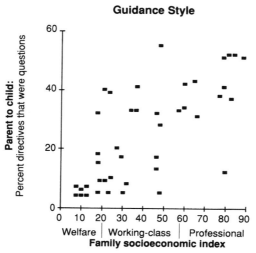

Figure 16. Each square is the characteristic Guidance Style of an individual parent's interactions. (See Appendix B for a detailed explanation of this figure.)

Responsiveness

Responsiveness denotes the relative amount of a child's experience with controlling the course of interaction. Parent responses reflect a parent's interest in supporting and encouraging a child's practice and the parent's appreciation of, and adaptation to, the child's current skill level and choice of topic. Responsiveness is at the core of teaching at the zone of proximal development. To exemplify Responsiveness, we used the proportion of all parent responses that were not preceded by parent initiations. From the number of all parent responses to the child per hour we subtracted the number of parent initiations to the child per hour and divided the result by all parent responses.

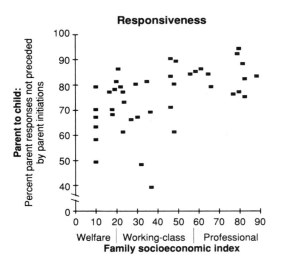

Figure 17.   Each square is the characteristic Responsiveness of an individual parent's interactions. (See Appendix B for a detailed explanation of this figure.)

Amount of Significant Family
Experience and Accomplishments at Age 3

All five variables exemplifying the categories of significant family experience, like the measures of the quality features of language and interaction from which they were derived, were highly related to one another, to family SES, and to all child accomplishments at age 3. Data for each of the parents and children are listed in Table 3[4] and shown graphically in Figures 13–17. We used multiple regression analyses to see which derived variables were related to child accomplishments beyond their common correlations.

We found that Language Diversity and Feedback Tone were somewhat independent of one another and differently related to child accomplishments at age 3. Language Diversity was more strongly related to child vocabulary use at age 3. Feedback Tone was more strongly related to rate of vocabulary growth and general accomplishments estimated by IQ score. Language Diversity and Feedback Tone may be seen as characterizing the fundamental quality of a child's everyday experience with language and interaction. The greater the amount of Language Diversity in parent talk, the more opportunities the child has for observational learning about how words refer and how they are used in relation to other words. The more positive the affect during interactions the more motivated the child is to explore new topics, to try out tentative relationships, to listen and practice, to add words to those already accumulated, and to notice the facts and relationships that IQ testers ask about.

Symbolic Emphasis, Guidance Style, and Responsiveness, when compared with each other, seemed to identify characteristics of language and interaction that

Table 3. Categories of significant family experience before age 3, children's accomplishments at age 3, and performance at age 9

Rank by SEI	Experience before age 3					Children at age 3			Scores at age 9–10	
	Language diversity	Feedback tone	Symbolic emphasis	Guidance style	Responsiveness	Vocabulary growth	Vocabulary use	IQ	PPVT–R	TOLD
1	134	.77	.98	.51	.83	7.40	269	139		
2	172	.94	1.00	.52	.82	7.67	375	126		
3	103	.89	.68	.37	.75	7.35	292	110	112	56
4	165	.90	.87	.52	.88	7.33	280	105	116	73
5	161	.96	.88	.51	.77	7.08	247	113	134	70
6	177	.83	.75	.12	.94	7.52	401	115	113	65
7	186	.85	.93	.41	.92	7.06	274	122		
8	175	.93	.92	.38	.76	7.00	204	110		
9	95	.87	.87	.31	.79	7.58	368	120	114	74
10	112	.90	.78	.43	.84	7.59	270	115		
11	171	.79	.80	.42	.86	7.42	285	108		
12	138	.73	.81	.34	.85	7.21	281	127	94	65
13	155	.82	1.00	.33	.84	7.49	317	108	102	65
14	185	.89	1.10	.55	.89	7.67	368	149	116	76
15	13	.21	.40	.05	.61	6.75	182	98	95	44
16	82	.73	.78	.28	.80	7.42	267	122	122	71
17	191	.71	.78	.13	.90	7.25	293	93	94	65
18	62	.55	.62	.17	.71	7.08	212	120	95	62
19	127	.82	.81	.32	.83	7.42	250	113	112	63
20	66	.52	.67	.41	.39	7.47	246	105	116	64
21	83	.55	.99	.33	.69	7.04	256	129	121	69
22	113	.84	.77	.33	.81	7.03	238	98	102	55
23	70	.42	.66	.08	.48	6.61	179	96	79	48
24	32	.83	.46	.05	.67	6.78	107	108	86	55
25	72	.68	.72	.17	.80	6.97	200	90		
26	98	.62	.63	.20	.66	6.15	89	62	105	54
27	40	.46	.57	.10	.73	6.71	132	98		

28	56	.29	.52	.05	.61	6.31	126	93	80	48
29	141	.70	.97	.39	.77	7.21	241	139	108	47
30	62	.46	.55	.09	.79	6.41	107	103	127	77
31	147	.70	.82	.40	.86	7.32	318	122	86	66
32	53	.51	.44	.09	.81	6.90	198	96	105	66
33	25	.39	.51	.05	.68	7.03	249	109	96	60
34	66	.59	.58	.15	.78	7.01	210	113		
35	66	.86	.57	.18	.70	6.93	189	93		
36	149	.47	.88	.32	.77	[a]	311	113	105	59
37	60	.58	.50	.07	.79	6.93	221	103	79	40
38	20	.21	.52	.07	.63	6.52	131	75		
39	29	.39	.62	.04	.49	6.71	139	74		
40	46	.20	.52	.04	.67	6.65	159	74		
41	40	.15	.47	.04	.70	6.64	123	84	83	43
42	58	.23	.63	.06	.58	6.56	120	66	76	48
Average:	100	.64	.72	.25	.75	7.05	232	106	103	60
r with:										
SES	.68	.73	.62	.71	.50	.65	.63	.54	*	*
Language diversity	—	.73	.84	.76	.70	.64	.73	.53	*	.59
Feedback tone		—	.67	.75	.64	.71	.64	.58	.59	.64
Symbolic emphasis			—	.76	*	.69	.72	.67	.64	.70
Guidance style				—	*	.73	.67	.68	.77	.71
Responsiveness					—	.55	.62	.52	ns	*
r with:										
Vocabulary growth						—	.92	.73	.58	.74
Vocabulary use							—	.70	.57	.72
Stanford-Binet IQ								—	*	.64

Note: Numbers, p <.001; *, p .001< .01; ns, not significant. For an explanation of this table, see this chapter, endnote 4.

[a]Child 36 was an outlier who was not included in the analyses of vocabulary growth; see this chapter, endnote 4.

in somewhat different ways refined and added nuances to the fundamental amount and tone of children's experience. Symbolic Emphasis was more strongly related to vocabulary use, whereas Guidance Style was more strongly related to vocabulary growth and IQ score. Responsiveness was independently related to all three child accomplishments.

The analyses suggested that parents who provide more of the fundamentals, larger amounts of diverse language experience and more encouragement to learn, tend also to add the nuances. They tend to be responsive: They listen and prompt relative to what the child has to say more often than they try to interest the child in adult concerns. They tend to encourage autonomy: They ask for compliance more often than they demand it. They tend to make language important: They name and explain everything whether or not the child cares or understands (yet).

The socioeconomic status of the children's families could account for 42% of the variance in the children's rates of vocabulary growth ($r = .65$), 40% of the variance in their vocabulary use ($r = .63$), and 29% of the variance in their IQ test scores ($r = .54$) when they were 3 years old.

When we entered as "Parenting" all five derived variables in a multiple regression analysis with each of the child accomplishments at 3, the five categories of significant family experience with language and interaction could together account for 61% of the variance in the rates of vocabulary growth and in the vocabulary use of the 42 children ($r = .78$), and for 59% of the variance in their general accomplishments as estimated by the Stanford-Binet IQ score ($r = .77$). (See Figure 18.)

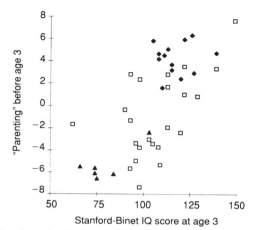

Figure 18.   Parenting is the combination of Language Diversity, Feedback Tone, Symbolic Emphasis, Guidance Style, and Responsiveness.
Each square is an individual parent's parenting before the child was age 3
plotted against the child's IQ test score at age 3. (See Appendix B for a detailed explanation of this figure.)

We had found what we were looking for in the longitudinal study: We saw that what parents said and did
with their children in the first 3 years of language learning had an enormous impact on how much language
their children learned and used. But the correlations
were not perfect; clearly, factors we had not included in
our analyses were influencing the children's accomplishments at 3. We wondered whether the differences we
saw at 3 would be washed out, like the effects of a
preschool intervention, as the children's experience
broadened to a wider community of competent speakers.
Like the parents we observed, we wondered how much
difference children's early experiences would actually
make. Could we, or parents, predict how a child would

do in school from what the parent was doing when the child was 2 years old?

Test Performance in
Third Grade and Accomplishments at Age 3

Fortune provided us with Dale Walker, who recruited 29 of the 42 families to participate in a study of their children's school performance. When the children were in the third grade, Dr. Walker provided us with their scores on a battery of standardized tests.[5] We had a chance to see the extent to which the children's language accomplishments at 3, and their experience with language and interaction at the age of 1–2 years, would predict their academic performance at age 9–10 years, after 6–7 years of intervening experience.

We were awestruck at how well our measures of accomplishments at 3 predicted measures of language skill at 9–10 (see Table 3). From our preschool data we had been confident that rate of vocabulary growth would predict later performance in school; we saw that it does. For the 29 children observed when they were 1–2 years old, rate of vocabulary growth at age 3 was strongly associated with scores at age 9–10 on both the Peabody Picture Vocabulary Test–Revised (PPVT–R) of receptive vocabulary ($r = .58$) and the Test of Language Development–2: Intermediate (TOLD) ($r = .74$) and its subtests (listening, speaking, semantics, syntax).

Vocabulary use at 3 was equally predictive of measures of language skill at age 9–10. Vocabulary use at 3 was strongly associated with score on both the PPVT–R ($r = .57$) and the TOLD ($r = .72$). Vocabulary use at 3 was also strongly associated with reading comprehension score on the Comprehensive Test of Basic Skills

(CTBS/U) (r = .56). General competence as estimated by Stanford-Binet IQ test score at 3 less strongly predicted scores on both the PPVT–R and the TOLD (r = .64), presumably because only part of the Stanford-Binet IQ test is related to language.

We had speculated, however, that rates of vocabulary growth might be related rather specifically to language skills. We saw no association between rate of vocabulary growth and the children's third-grade scores in the academic skill areas of reading, writing, spelling, and arithmetic or with scores on the Otis-Lennon School Ability Test, 6th edition (OLSAT) of verbal and nonverbal reasoning.[6] Nor was any association seen between either vocabulary use or IQ test score at 3 and performance in these other academic skill areas at 9–10.

Early Family Experience and Test Performance in Third Grade

Given the predictability of child accomplishments at age 9–10 from accomplishments at age 3, we asked whether we could also predict the children's accomplishments at 9–10 from what their parents had been doing 6 or 7 years earlier when the children were 1–2 years old. We found that our derived variables predicted scores on the TOLD almost as well as did child accomplishments at 3: Language Diversity (r = .59), Feedback Tone (r = .64), Symbolic Emphasis (r = .70), and Guidance Style (r = .71) were strongly associated with scores on the TOLD. Feedback Tone (r = .59), Symbolic Emphasis (r = .64), and Guidance Style (r = .77) were better predictors of scores on the PPVT–R than were child accomplishments at 3. Responsiveness was weakly associated with scores on the TOLD but not with scores on the PPVT–R, and there were no strong associations between the derived variables and performance in other academic skill areas.

As a strong test of the data and our efforts to summarize what we had observed these 29 parents actually doing with their children, we compared the derived variables to family SES to see which could account for more of the variance in children's performance on third-grade tests of language skill 6 years later. Family SES could account for 30% of the variance in the children's PPVT–R scores ($r = .55$) and 24% of the variance in their TOLD scores ($r = .49$) in the third grade. A multiple regression analysis showed that the five derived variables exemplifying categories of significant family experience before age 3 could together account for 61% of the variance in the children's scores on both the PPVT–R and the TOLD ($rs = .78$). The link between the parents' income, education, and social status and their children's academic test performance had declined by the third grade. However, the link between what the parents were doing with their children before the children were 3 years old remained as strong as ever over the intervening 6 years ($p < .001$).

Vocabulary Growth Revisited

We returned to our 20-year-old questions, those that had brought us to the longitudinal observations, and we looked again at the data from the Turner House children and the professors' children. We compared the extremes we had observed in the preschool to the extremes among the 42 families—the welfare children (all of whom would have been eligible for the Turner House Preschool program when it existed) and the children in professional families, even though it meant comparing data from different sources, years, and child ages.

The data from the professors' children and the Turner House children were recorded during preschool free play rather than during interactions at home. The children were 5 years old at the end of the preschool year and were all competent speakers rather than just beginning to accumulate vocabulary. We were comparing children in families separated by 15 years of social and economic changes in society, a fact brought home to us when we recruited in the longitudinal study a parent whom we had taught in the Turner House Preschool when she was 4.

Nevertheless, test scores from the two groups were surprisingly comparable. The 12 professors' children were tested in 1967 at an average age of 5:2; their average score on the PPVT was 117. The average Stanford-Binet IQ score of the 13 children observed in professional families was 117 at age 3. The 11 Turner House children were tested in 1967 at an average age of 4:11; their average score on the PPVT was 75. The average Stanford-Binet IQ score at age 3 of the 6 welfare children observed at home was 79.

In 1967 we did not have the sophisticated statistical model of vocabulary growth developed by Dr. Thissen (see this chapter, endnote 1). In his multilevel nonlinear model, vocabulary growth began at the first recorded word and increased with each monthly observation independent of the amount of talking the children did. Our vocabulary growth curves in 1967 were cumulative type/token curves[7] (see Figure 1) that described the rate the Turner House and professors' children were using words from previously learned vocabulary. An estimate

163

of vocabulary resources is gained from such curves only after 10,000 or more spoken words have been recorded.

We derived an average growth slope from the data we had used to construct the cumulative type/token curves of the Turner House and the professors' children. Between 10,000 and 15,000 spoken words, the average growth slope for the Turner House children was .027 or 3 new words added to the dictionary in use per 100 words spoken. The average growth slope for the professors' children was .060 or 6 new words added to the dictionary in use per 100 words spoken. The vocabularies in use by the professors' children were growing at twice the rate of the vocabularies in use by the Turner House children.

For the children in welfare and professional families in the longitudinal study, we compared the number of new words added to the recorded vocabulary between the ages of 30–36 months, when all the children were regularly using sentences and clauses appropriately. The welfare children added an average of 168 words in the 6 months from age 30–36 months; the children in professional families added an average of 350 or twice as many. The welfare children were adding fewer numbers of words to vocabularies already smaller: At 30 months, the welfare children had an average recorded vocabulary of 357 words, less than half as many as the 766 words in the average vocabulary of the children in professional families.

Like the children in the Turner House Preschool, the welfare children at age 3 not only had smaller vocabularies than did children of the same age in professional families, but they were also adding words more slowly (compare Figures 1 and 2). Projecting the developmental trajectory of the welfare children's vocabulary growth curves, we could see an ever-widening gap similar to the one we saw between the Turner House children and the professors' children in 1967. And the children's PPVT–R scores in third grade showed us how unlikely the gap was to narrow with increasing years of experience.

Everyday Parenting Revisited

We now had answers to our 20-year-old questions. We had observed, recorded, and analyzed more than 1,300 hours of casual interactions between parents and their language-learning children. We had disassembled these interactions into several dozen molecular features that could be reliably coded and counted. We had examined the correlations between the quantities of each of those features and several outcome measures relating to children's language accomplishments. Based on those correlations, our understanding of the literature, and the impressions concerning stable patterns of parenting we had absorbed from thousands of hours of observing different families similarly raising children, we reassembled the quality features into five derived variables that exemplified the categories of significant family experience we had seen occurring in all family homes.

We saw that each of the five derived variables was more strongly related to children's accomplishments than were most of the molecular variables, the particular quality features of language and interaction, of which they were composed. Each of the five variables derived to exemplify categories of significant family experiences was strongly related to family SES: We saw the immense gulf between the amount and richness of daily experience separating children's lives at the extremes of advantage.

The relationship between each of the five derived variables and family SES has been shown in Figures

13–17. The strong relationship between the amount of each derived variable and family SES is apparent: Overall, the higher the SES, the greater the amount of each derived variable. At the extremes, we see nearly all the advantaged children receiving from their college-educated professional parents large amounts of each derived variable and nearly all the children being raised in welfare homes receiving small amounts of each variable from their isolated parents. In the middle we see the marked variety of the American working class: Some families are high and some are low in terms of the amounts of the categories of significant family experience they provide their children, and there is no relationship to the status of their jobs.

We turned to the other question that had led us to the longitudinal study, which was our need to know about children's early experience not just at the extremes in advantage but across the full spectrum of American families. If the variables we derived from our observations of children at home were important characteristics of family experience and not just epiphenomenal correlates of other "real" variables associated with SES, we should see the effects of these variables relative to the accomplishments of the 23 children in the working-class families where the correlations between the derived variables and SES were nearly zero.

The Language Diversity of the talk that the 23 working-class parents addressed to their children was not significantly related to their SES or to the children's IQ scores, but it was somewhat related to their children's vocabulary growth and was strongly related to their children's vocabulary use. Feedback Tone in the 23 working-class families was not significantly related to their SES, to the children's IQ scores, or to their vocabulary use and was only somewhat related to their children's vocabulary growth. Symbolic Emphasis in the speech of the 23 working-class parents was not significantly related to their SES and was somewhat related to their children's vocabulary growth, but was strongly related to their children's vocabulary use and IQ test scores. Guidance Style in the 23 working-class families was not related to their SES but was strongly related to the vocabulary growth, vocabulary use, and IQ test scores of their children. The Responsiveness of the working-class parents was not related to either SES or to any of the children's accomplishments at 3.

Overall the socioeconomic status of the 23 working-class families could not account for a significant amount of their children's accomplishments at age 3 or for the test scores of the 19 working-class children at age 9 in the third grade. But parenting, all five derived variables when entered in a multiple regression analysis could together account for over 60% of the variance in the measures of accomplishment at age 3 (vocabulary growth, vocabulary use, and Stanford-Binet IQ score) and in the PPVT–R and TOLD scores at age 9–10. These relationships are summarized in Table 4.

The five derived variables, which so uniformly marked the SES extremes among the families we observed, also robustly predicted the accomplishments of the working-class children, and race made no contribution to the prediction.[8] We conclude that these variables are not simply marker variables denoting social class or subculture but are powerful characteristics of everyday parenting that cause important outcomes in children (see Figure 18). We had succeeded in capturing in the data the categories of significant family experience we had seen blended in the everyday parenting we observed in all 42 families. Some

Table 4. Correlations between children's accomplishments and family SES and parenting

	Vocabulary growth at age 3		Vocabulary use at age 3		IQ test score at age 3		PPVT score at age 9		TOLD score at age 9	
	All SES[a]	Working class	All SES	Working class	All SES	Working class	All SES	Working class	All SES	Working class
$n^b =$	41	22	42	23	42	23	29	19	29	19
SES	.65**	.46	.63**	.31	.54**	.24	.55*	.19	.49*	.15
Parenting[c]	.78**	.74**	.78**	.80**	.77**	.76**	.78**	.82**	.78**	.75**

*$p < .01$ ** $p < .001$

[a]All SES = professional, welfare, and working class.

[b]See text for explanation of differences in the number of children included in each analysis. Data for individual children and families are shown in Table 3. The outlier, Child 36, was not included in the analyses of vocabulary growth; see this chapter, endnote 4.

[c]Parenting = all five categories of significant family experience combined.

categories were more characteristic of parenting in some SES groups and less characteristic of parenting in others, but the amount of whatever combination was characteristic of everyday parenting in the individual family was predictive of the accomplishments of the child.

From the tremendous effort we had put into the years of observing ordinary families and coding the resulting volume of data we learned about what is happening to children at home and the experiences that influence their developmental trajectories. But we also learned that the problem of intervening in the lives of children from families in poverty is considerably more complex than we thought, simply because the first 3 years of experience are so much more important than we thought.

Endnotes

1. Dr. David Thissen, director of the Psychometric Labora-
    tory at the University of North Carolina, is an expert in
    the statistical measurement of growth curves (see Thissen
    & Bock, 1990). He used the month-by-month increments
    in the recorded vocabulary for each of the children we ob-
    served to fit a nonlinear curve to each child's cumulative
    vocabulary growth and from these derived a "normal"
    curve of expressive vocabulary growth.

    His multilevel model of vocabulary growth has three
    parameters:

    a) a "slope" parameter reflecting the rate-of-vocabu-
    lary-acquisition at the maximum rate of acquisition. The
    age at this maximum rate varies for individual children,
    but those with large values on the "slope" parameter are
    acquiring words faster.

    b) a "location" parameter reflecting the age at which a
    maximum rate of vocabulary growth is achieved (after
    some acceleration, before deceleration). (The average age
    of the 42 children at this "location" was 29 months, range
    23–32 months.)

    c) an "asymptote" parameter reflecting where the rate
    of growth is going, on the scale of the logarithm of the
    number of words. The "asymptote" does not imply an end
    or slowing of word learning but rather the number of
    words acquired in this early phase.

    Further work with the statistical aspects of the model
    was reported by McFarlane (1994).

2. The vocabulary data from the children were coded and
    computer processed exactly as were the data from the par-
    ents. An individual dictionary was compiled for each
    child, and it was checked at each observation in order to
    add new entries and count the different words appearing
    in the child's utterances. The reliability of child words
    was assessed exactly as the reliability of parent words (see
    Chapter 6, endnote 3) when each observer listened inde-

pendently to the randomly chosen tapes on each child she had not observed and marked on the transcript each word she agreed she heard on the tape. As in that assessment, the observer marked disagreements on individual words, on utterance segmentation, and added omitted words to total disagreements. Agreements were divided by the totals reported by computer processing of the observation. Average agreement was .95 (range .79–1.00 per child).

Menard and Santerre (1979) reported a large-scale study of adults in Canada who were asked to speak onto audiotape; they found that speech richer in vocabulary, especially nouns and modifiers, marked individuals with more education, higher-salaried jobs, and more affluent areas of residence.

3. Each child was administered the Stanford-Binet IQ test (Terman & Merrill, 1960) within a month after the final observation at age 3. A professional psychologist not associated with the longitudinal research gave each child the test.

Weinberg (1989) summarized the years of study and argument concerning what intelligence is, whether it is, how it might develop, and what IQ tests seem to be measuring.

4. Table 3 shows for each of the 42 children the five categories of significant family experience before age 3, accomplishments at age 3, and performance at age 9–10. Rank is the same as in Appendix A. Correlation coefficients are shown only if they were significant at the .001 level; asterisks indicate correlations with significant levels between .001 and .01. At age 3 the 42 children were observed at home; at age 9–10, 29 of the 42 children were tested in school (see this chapter, endnote 5).

The categories of significant family experience before 3 are the derived variables, Language Diversity, Feedback Tone, Symbolic Emphasis, Guidance Style, and Responsiveness. Language Diversity indicates the parent's propensity to talk in varied contexts, as exemplified by the average total number of different nouns and modifiers the parent used. Feedback Tone indicates how proportionately affirmative the parent's feedback was to the child, as exemplified by the average amount of affirmative feedback divided by all feedback, affirmative plus prohibitions. Symbolic Emphasis indicates the importance of precise language in family interactions, as exemplified by the average number of nouns, modifiers, and past-tense verbs the parent used per utterance. Guidance Style indicates the parent's propensity to ask the child rather than to demand behavior, as exemplified by the proportion of auxiliary-fronted yes/no questions ("Can you. . .") in total requests (auxiliary-fronted yes/no questions plus imperatives). Responsiveness indicates the relative importance during interaction of the child's behavior, as exemplified by the average proportion of all parent responses that were not preceded by parent initiations (parent responses minus parent initiations divided by parent responses).

Child accomplishments at 3 were vocabulary growth, which is the projection of the vocabulary growth curve in Thissen's multilevel model (see this chapter, endnote 1); vocabulary use, which is the average number of different words the child used in the last three (34–36 months of age) observations (see this chapter, endnote 2); and Stanford-Binet IQ scores (see this chapter, endnote 3).

In the regression analyses in which vocabulary growth was the dependent variable, the data of only 41 of the 42 children were used. The average age at which the children began to talk was 11 months. The child ranked 36 waited until the age of 24 months before beginning to talk; the parameters of this child's vocabulary growth curve are multivariate outliers. Therefore, so that the regression analysis would better represent the group as a whole, this child's vocabulary growth curve was set aside for separate consideration.

Children's scores at ages 9–10 are those of the 29 children tested in third grade (see this chapter, endnote 5). PPVT–R is the Peabody Picture Vocabulary Test–Revised (Dunn & Dunn, 1981). TOLD is the Test of Language Development–2: Intermediate (Hammill & Newcomer, 1988).

5. Dale Walker of the University of Kansas conducted the follow-up study as part of the research program of the Juniper Gardens Children's Project in Kansas City, Kansas, sponsored by the University of Kansas Schiefelbusch Institute for Life Span Studies. See Walker, Greenwood, Hart, and Carta (1994) for a description of the methods and results of the study. Children were individually tested in the spring and fall of each year from kindergarten to third grade. When tested in the spring of third grade some children were 9 years old and some were 10. The tests given were: Peabody Picture Vocabulary Test–Revised (PPVT–R) (Dunn & Dunn, 1981), a test of receptive one-word vocabulary in response to pictures; Test of Language Development–2: Intermediate (TOLD) (Hammill & Newcomer, 1988), a test of spoken language consisting of sentence combining, how words are alike, word ordering, word categories, grammatical comprehension, and malapropisms; Wide Range Achievement Test–Revised (WRAT–R) (Jastak & Wilkinson, 1984), a test used to assess spelling achievement; The Comprehensive Test of Basic Skills (CTBS/U 3rd ed.) (CTBS, 1987), a test used to assess reading, writing, and arithmetic; and Otis-Lennon School Ability Test 6th edition (OLSAT) (Otis & Lennon, 1989), a test designed to assess verbal comprehension, verbal reasoning, and pictorial, figural, and quantitative reasoning.

Dr. Walker obtained permission for testing from the schools the children attended and from the children's parents. Of the 42 children, 29 were in the follow-up group tested in third grade. Three of the families had moved out of the city, and 3 of the children in the welfare families at age 3 could not be located in the city schools. Six of the professional and one of the working-class parents declined by saying they did not want their children to feel they were being singled out from their classmates; unlike many of the parents who gave permission, these parents expressed little interest in additional documentation that their children were achieving academically.

The subset of children tested in school was more homogeneous and more middle class than the group of 42 families. The 29 children included only half of the children observed in the professional and welfare families but 83% of the children observed in working-class families. For this subset of 29 children, though, we saw the same strong relationships between the measures of accomplishment at age 3. Vocabulary growth rate was strongly associated with vocabulary use ($r = .92$), and both were strongly associated with general accomplishments as estimated by Stanford-Binet IQ score ($rs = .69$ and $.72$). The association of vocabulary growth and vocabulary use with SES was somewhat less strong ($rs = .60$ and $.59$), and IQ score was not associated with family SES.

6. We saw no association between children's accomplishments at age 3 (rate of vocabulary growth, vocabulary use, IQ score) and achievement in third grade in academic skill areas other than those specifically related to language. Whether there would be an association later in elementary school or in high school when so much of the curriculum begins to depend on vocabulary resources (see Becker, 1977), we do not yet know.

7. We discussed the comparison of the Turner House children's growth curves and issues related to cumulative vocabulary growth and its measurement in Hart and Risley (1981).

8. Among the 23 working-class families, 10 were African American and 13 were white. Multiple regression analyses showed that race made no contribution to any of the child accomplishments over and above parenting. A separate regression analysis was run for vocabulary growth, vocabulary use, and IQ; in each we controlled for parenting by entering the sum of the z scores for the five derived variables first and then entering race. In each analysis the change in r square was less than or equal to .01 and nonsignificant.

173

CHAPTER EIGHT

The Importance of the First 3 Years of Family Experience

❖ ❖ ❖ ❖

As we observed the everyday parenting characteristic of individual families, we were impressed with how parents in casually socializing with their children gave them hour after hour of experience with the quality features of language and interaction. We were equally impressed with how completely the children relied on their families to provide that experience. We realized how unique the first 3 years are in the lives of humans just because infants are so utterly dependent on adults for all their nurture and knowledge.

Before children can take charge of their own experience and begin to spend time with peers in social groups outside the home, almost everything they learn comes from their families, to whom society has assigned the task of socializing children. We were not surprised to see the 42 children turn out to be like their parents; we had not fully realized, however, the implications of those similarities for the children's futures.

Children Behave Like Their Parents

We observed the 42 children grow more like their parents in stature and activity levels, in vocabulary resources, and in language and interaction styles. Despite the considerable range in vocabulary size among the children, 86%–98% of the words recorded in each child's vocabulary consisted of words also recorded in their parents' vocabularies. The size of the children's recorded vocabularies and their IQ scores were strongly associated with the size of their parents' recorded vocabularies ($r = .77$) and the parents' scores on a vocabulary pretest ($r = .70$).[1] By the age of 34–36 months, the children were also talking and using numbers of different words very similar to the averages of their parents (see Table 5).

We could see heredity and family experience so intermingled as to make the differences that we saw between the children in later school performance even less surprising. By the time the children were 3 years old, trends in amount of talk, vocabulary growth, and style of

Table 5.   Averages for measures of parent and child language and test scores

	Families					
	13 Professional		23 Working-class		6 Welfare	
Measures and scores	Parent	Child	Parent	Child	Parent	Child
Pretest score[a]	41		31		14	
IQ score at age 3		117		107		79
Recorded vocabulary size	2,176	1,116	1,498	749	974	525
Average utterances per hour[b]	487	310	301	223	176	168
Average different words per hour	382	297	251	216	167	149

[a]See this chapter, endnote 1, for description of the pretest and testing conditions.

[b]Parent utterances and different words were averaged over 13–36 months of child age. Child utterances and different words were averaged for the four observations when the children were 33–36 months old.

interaction were well established. Even patterns of parenting were already observable among the children. When we listened to the children, we seemed to hear their parents speaking; when we watched the children play at parenting their dolls, we seemed to see the futures of their own children.

We compared the Feedback Tone of the children's utterances at 3 with their family experience. We looked at how generally affirmative the interactions were among other family members when the children were 13–18 months old, before they were saying more than occasional words, and then at how affirmative the children themselves were at age 3.[2] We saw that in the working-class families about half of all feedback was affirmative among family members when the child was 13–18 months old; similarly, about half the feedback given by the child at 34–36 months was affirmative. In the professional families, slightly more than half of the feedback exchanged among parents and siblings was affirmative, but more than 80% of the feedback to the 13- to 18-month-old child was affirmative. When the children in the professional families were 34–36 months old, almost 70% of the feedback they gave to other family members was affirmative.

Just as the children in the professional families at age 3 shared the prevailing affirmative tone of family interactions, the children in the welfare families at age 3 shared the prevailing negative tone. Almost 80% of the welfare parents' feedback to their 13- to 18-month-old children was negative; almost 80% of the children's feedback to family members when they were 34–36 months old was negative. But an average of more than 90% of parent feedback to the children's older siblings, and 85% of the feedback exchanged between family members,

177

was negative. A consistent and pervasive negative Feedback Tone was the model for the children of how families work together. Given the strong relationships shown in the longitudinal data between the prevalence of prohibitions in the first years of life and lowered child accomplishments, lasting still at age 9, the prospects for the next generation of welfare children seem bleak.

The frequency and tone of the interactions in the welfare families limited the words and meanings the children heard. Because the welfare parents talked less often to their children, they talked in less varied contexts about less varied aspects of the children's experience. Because they spent less time interacting with their children, they had fewer opportunities to learn about their children's skill levels and the topics the children were interested in talking and hearing about. Perhaps as a result, proportionately more of their talk contained prohibitions and simple directives. When the parents did take time to talk to their children, they provided their children experience with language proportionally as rich in quality features as the language provided by working-class parents. They just took the time less often.

Intergenerational Transmission of Family Culture

The most impressive aspects of the longitudinal data are how different individual families and children are and how much and how important is children's cumulative experience before age 3. Although we found SES categories useful for contrasting the extremes in advantage and for summarizing characteristic patterns of language and interaction, we saw in the families themselves the blending of parenting styles characteristic of a classless society. We saw the patterns of language and interaction of the professional parents in equal quantity in some working-class families; in other working-class families the children's lives looked very similar to those of the children in the welfare families.

We could see in the professional families the American dream: parents adding to and handing on to their children the advantages their families had given to them. We saw the daily efforts of these parents to transmit an educationally advantaged culture to their children through the display of enriched language; through the amount of talking they did and how informative they were; and through the frequency of gentle guidance, affirmative interactions, and responsiveness to their children's talk. They represented the success stories we saw motivating the efforts of many of the working-class families.

We could see in the diversity of the working-class families the nation's wealth in originality. In these families we saw a rich mixture of styles: parents who combined frequent prohibitions with lots of affirmatives and parents who seldom gave their children feedback of any kind; parents who were more responsive and talkative than many of the professional parents and parents who responded and talked as little as some of the welfare parents. We saw the varied motivations of the working-class families: parents who interacted with their children much as the professional parents did, preparing their children for the culture they intended their children to attain, and the working poor struggling just to make life a little better for themselves and their children.

We could see in the welfare families the nation's continuing failure to eradicate poverty. We saw the welfare parents' isolation from the world of working-class parents and from opportunities to see and talk about the parenting styles that were providing so much more cumulative experience to the average classmates the welfare children would meet in school. We saw poverty of experience being transmitted across generations. The welfare children, like the other children after the first 3 years of experience at home, had become like their parents. We wondered that we could have thought their accomplishments at 3 would be other than similar to those of their parents. We could see too why a few hours of intensive intervention at age 4 had had so little impact on the magnitude of the differences in cumulative experience that resulted from those first 3 years.

The First Years of Life

The first years of life are overwhelmingly important because not only survival but all of an infant's experience of the world depends on other people. We need not take the position that the first 3 years are *the* most important time, only that the first 3 years are a time when children are uniquely susceptible to the culture of adults, before interaction with peers and the social standards of schools become important influences on what children learn.

The helplessness of human infants makes them both particularly vulnerable and especially malleable. Research continues to demonstrate how fine are the auditory and visual discriminations infants can make in the very first months of life. We know that by age 2 the growth and mylenization of nerve cells is almost complete and that by age 4 cortical development is largely finished. We know that physical development, once complete, becomes less vulnerable to external forces; if the same is true of neurological development, the years before 2 are the time when environmental stimulation may have the greatest impact on cortical development.

Within the varied activities parents arranged for their children, we could see a curriculum of planned experiences, society's agenda for transforming the amorphous, amoral behavior of a newborn into the skilled self-sufficiency of a 3-year-old. Society delegates to parents the implementation of this child-rearing curriculum and gives them almost complete control over the presentation, timing, and sequencing of experiences; intervention is acceptable only in cases of abuse or neglect. Society relies for stability on the intergenerational transmission of competence and assumes that all adult participants in the social group can provide children with the necessary experiences.

We could marvel at the diversity of successful individuals produced by so many variations on a standard curriculum for socializing children. But what we were seeing as minor variations, the children were experiencing as the entirety of normal family life. Nearly everything the children saw and heard was conditional on their parents; everything they knew about the structure of the interpersonal world was referenced to their own experience in the family.

Society supplies the curriculum and its goals; the nature of infancy and of the species ensure that these will be learned. Infants are born with physical and cognitive capacities that support active exploration and engage with every change in sensory experience. Observational learning allows social groups to model the ways of society and wait for infants to do what they see everyone else in the world doing. Dependency assures that parents are the source of everything important to infants: food, comfort, love, models of success and maturity. Interaction provides practice in the social dance of the family.

Net and Proportional Amounts of Experience

Given the nature of babies and their interactions, the very first years of life establish an entire general approach to experience. A vocabulary of how things are done is laid down in interactions with an adult about things that matter. Children learn through words and actions what the world means, who they are, and what is valued. Children learn what it means to be a social being, how to use language, and the patterns of what people do interpersonally.

For infants, amount of experience entails variety of experience. More is better because in infancy everything is novel and interesting; narrowing comes with socialization, as children learn to fit into the standards and practices of the social group. Infants are so curious and so easily distracted, and their knowledge is so limited, that everything their parents do and say expands their experience. Growth and development are so rapid and infants' attention spans are so short that parents are responding to behaviors varying as continually as the contexts in which they occur. A cumulative vocabulary of the meanings that will be available for thinking and acting grows with the net amount of experience.

From proportional amounts of experience, children learn about their own and other people's characteristics and traits. Part of the vocabulary of meanings children learn are words such as *good, pretty, mean, ugly,* and *liar.* Children accumulate both net and proportional amounts of experience hearing their parents use these words. If, for example, a child hears her parent use the word *pretty* 50 times and the word *homely* only 5 times, the child will have differing amounts of net experience with the two words and so accumulate a larger vocabulary of meanings associated with *pretty* than with *homely*. However, if of the 50 times the child hears the word *pretty* it is used only 5 times to refer to her rather than to a sibling, and all 5 times she hears the word *homely* it is used to refer to her, the child learns about a personal characteristic.

From proportional amounts of experience, children learn a vocabulary for comparing themselves to others and for describing who they are. This proportional experience continually adds up, accumulating as a kind of lifetime batting average, ending up as the self-concept that influences expectations for success and motivation to try. Although later experience may provide niches of success, arenas in which children can feel confident and good about themselves, these are unlikely to displace cumulative feelings of relative inferiority or incompetence.

Proportional and net amounts of experience are cumulative and mutually influence one another. The accomplishments of the higher-SES children are hardly surprising when we consider their cumulative experience: 3 years of enriched language and activities, 3 years of being told they were "right" and "good," and 3 years of frequently being chosen as more interesting to listen to and talk to than anyone else.

An Example of a Limited Amount of Experience

It is hard to convey the flavor of growing up with only a small net amount of experience because there is so little to describe. In an attempt to do so, we give an example of 1 hour of observation in a welfare home; we have included the sequence of all the mother's interactions with her child but have omitted the 50 child initiations to which the mother did not respond. Note the proportion of the mother's talk that contains negative feedback, the number of initiations relative to responses, and the prevalence of imperatives.

Much in the example is typical of what we observed in all the families: The child is busily engaged in exploration; there are things to play with (a ball, a toy stethoscope, a purse, coins); and the parent provides routine care, dressing, feeding, and changing the child. The contrast is in the *amount* of the child's experience: the number of opportunities the mother has to talk with the child that go unused. Nearly all the other mothers we observed would, for example, have tried to redirect the child's attention from the observer to feeding a doll; they would have talked about the stethoscope, played ball with the child, or asked whether she could count the coins.

> Inge's mother is sitting in the living room watching television. Inge (23 months) gets her mother's keys from the couch. Her mother initiates, "Bring them keys back here. You ain't going nowhere." Inge does not answer; she sits playing with the keys.
> Her mother initiates, "Inge, what you do with the money?" Inge goes and picks up off the floor the $5 paid for the observation. Her mother initiates, "Put it on the TV," and Inge does so, without saying anything.
> Inge gets a spoon from a coffee cup and "feeds" her mother, who says, "That's good. Thank you." Inge then holds out the spoon to the observer and her mother initiates, "Stop, Inge. No." Inge does not answer and her mother initiates, "Don't be rolling your eyes at me either."
> Playing with the spoon, Inge bangs it on the radio. Her mother initiates, "Hey, stop that. Don't beat on that radio." Inge babbles and points to the beach pictured on the

TV; her mother responds, "That's where we need to be, Inge." Inge says something incomprehensible, and her mother does not reply.

Inge drops the spoon on the coffee table. Her mother initiates, "O.K., now, leave it alone, O.K., Inge?" Inge does not answer; when she picks the spoon up again, her mother initiates, "Come here. Let me bite you if you gonna keep on meddling." Inge goes on playing; when she bangs the spoon on the coffee table, her mother initiates, "Inge, stop."

Inge goes to the observer and reaches for her equipment. Her mother initiates, "You can't meddle with her stuff." Her mother comments to the observer as Inge continues to reach and then initiates, "You better leave her alone." Inge continues, and her mother initiates, "Stop. Do I have to spank your little leg?" Inge answers, softly, "No." Her mother asks, "Huh?" and Inge replies, "No." Her mother says, "Well you better be good, O.K." Inge says, "O.K." Inge picks up a toy stethoscope, plays with it, drops it, and then gets her bottle off the coffee table. Her mother picks Inge up onto her lap without saying anything and then moves her beside her on the couch. Inge gets down and goes to the observer. Her mother initiates, "You just got to touch her, huh." Inge says, "Yeah." Her mother says, "Yeah. You better fix your clothes." Inge does not answer.

The mother leaves to go to the bathroom and Inge follows, saying something incomprehensible. Her mother says, "Go back Inge." Inge says, "No," and her mother says, "Don't be telling me, 'No.' Get back in there. I'ma spank you." Inge returns to the living room.

The mother returns; Inge sits on the couch beside her to watch TV and says something incomprehensible. Mother responds, "Quit copying off of me. You a copycat." Inge says something incomprehensible, and her mother does not respond.

Inge picks up her sister's purse from the couch. Her mother initiates, "You better get out of her purse." Inge continues to explore the purse and her mother initiates, "Get out of her purse." Inge does not answer; she begins to take coins out of the purse and put them on the coffee table. Her mother initiates, "Give me that purse." Inge continues to put coins on the table. Her mother initiates, "And the money." Inge does not answer but gives her mother the purse.

Inge says, "Potty"; her mother says, "You gotta potty?"and takes off Inge's diaper. Inge goes to the bathroom; her mother initiates, calling, "Are you finished, Inge?" When Inge returns to the living room her mother initiates, "Get a diaper," and when Inge does so her mother puts the diaper on.

Inge gets a ball and says, "Ball." Her mother says, "It's a ball." Inge says, "Ball," and her mother repeats, "Ball." When Inge throws the ball over by the TV as she repeats words from a commercial, her mother responds, "You know better. Why you do that?" Inge says something incomprehensible and her mother answers, "Don't throw it no more." Inge sits on the couch with the ball, gets down, and falls. Her mother initiates, "Now when you hurt yourself, then what?"

Inge gets back on the couch, stands, and then climbs over the back of the couch. Her mother initiates, "Hey quit climbing over my couch." She picks Inge up and kisses her. Holding Inge on her lap, her mother initiates, "Why you wanna be so bad? And don't be climbing up over there, hear? O.K.?" Inge does not answer.

Inge watches TV and initiates, "Lady." Her mother says, "She sleeping in the bed." Inge mumbles something, gets off the couch, and touches the observer. Her mother says, "Stop."

Her mother holds out Inge's shoe and initiates, "Get your little shoe on." Inge repeats, "Your little shoe," and her mother says, "Put your shoe on. Come here. You want this shoe on?" Inge says, "Yeah"; her mother puts the shoe on Inge without saying anything more. Inge looks around the room, saying something incomprehensible; her mother says, "Go look over there. It may be over there. Oh, here it is." Her mother shows Inge the ball. Inge says, "Give me. Ball give me." Her mother puts Inge's other shoe on without saying anything more.

Her mother leaves to go to the bedroom and Inge follows. The mother initiates, "Wanna take a bath?" Inge mutters something and her mother says, "I ain't never seen no baby don't wanna take a bath." Inge does not respond. They return to the living room; Inge gets the stethoscope and puts it in her ears; she walks around and then gets up on the couch and lies down. Her mother initiates, "Inge, you going to sleep, girl?" Inge does not answer.

This example of an hour of family life shows a mother who is concerned, nurturing, and affectionate; she holds standards for appropriate behavior, has toilet trained her child, dresses her, and holds and kisses her. She repeats the child's attempts at words ("ball"), and she tells the child about things ("She's sleeping in the bed."). But she makes few efforts to engage the child in conversation or to prompt the child to practice. She does not redirect or elaborate the child's initiatives; most of the feedback she gives is corrective or critical.

Cumulative Experience

The consistency of the data suggests that this child's everyday experience did not greatly differ over her first 3 years. The child's very small net amount of experience with language (relative to that of the average child) was joined with her proportional experience of being an individual not very "good" and not very interesting to the most important person in her life, the holder of all the knowledge and values of the culture. The child was as isolated as her mother was from other sources of knowledge and responses to her skills. We can speculate about

187

how much this child will actually know of the world, how it works, and what it contains when she is 3 years old and about how capable she will feel competing with her peers in school.

Our experiences in preschool intervention suggest that it will take thousands of hours of affirmative feedback even to begin to overcome what this child has learned about herself in her first 3 years. More thousands of hours will be required to give her the knowledge and the vocabulary of meanings of even the average children she will meet in school. And it is in the company of those better informed and more confident children that those innumerable experiences of success will have to be arranged.

Experience is cumulative; new experiences are recognized, added, and assimilated to past experiences or let go unnoticed or unnamed because there are no words and no past experiences with which to link them. The first 3 years may be the most important chiefly because changing what has been learned from past experience is so difficult and time consuming. After age 3, the unique circumstances for learning are gone; more vocabulary and knowledge have to be crammed in so as to expand the limits of what has become meaningful in experience. All this has to be done while encouraging feelings of being competent and interesting. It is not surprising that the task often seems hopeless once we have let the first 3 years of experience accumulate.

Endnotes

1. When we began the longitudinal study, in order to estimate the computer resources we would need for the parents' data, we asked the parents to complete a vocabulary pretest. At the first observation each parent was asked to complete a form abstracted from the Peabody Picture Vocabulary Test (PPVT) (Dunn, 1965). We gave each parent a list of 46 vocabulary words, those from the PPVT that would result for an 18-year-old in an IQ score between approximately 80 and 120 depending on the number of items correct. We gave each parent the series of pictures, four options per vocabulary word, and asked the parent to write beside each word the number of the picture that corresponded to the written word. The observers gave no help during the test or feedback after it. The conditions of testing do not permit any statements about IQ. Parent performance on the test was highly correlated with years of education $(r = .57)$.

2. We used data from the 25 children who had siblings present during observations when the children were 13–18 months old. We calculated Feedback Tone for the utterances recorded as addressed to those siblings (and any other relatives present) by the children's parents and for the utterances of the siblings to the parent and each other. Then we calculated Feedback Tone for the 25 children in the 34- to 36-month observations. We derived the proportion of all feedback that was affirmative (affirmative feedback divided by affirmative plus negative feedback) for each observation and averaged the results. We could not examine Responsiveness because we had not coded whether parent utterances to siblings were responses; most of the siblings and children were not sufficiently proficient to allow comparisons to their parents in Guidance Style and Symbolic Emphasis.

Intervention
to Equalize
Early Experience

❖ ❖ ❖ ❖

We undertook 2 1/2 years of observing 42 families for an hour each month to learn about
what typically went on in homes with 1- and
2-year-old children learning to talk. The data showed us
that ordinary families differ immensely in the amount of
experience with language and interaction they regularly
provide their children and that differences in children's
experience are strongly linked to children's language accomplishments both at age 3 and at age 9.

Our goal in the longitudinal study was to discover
what was happening in children's early experience that
could account for the intractable differences in rates of
vocabulary growth we saw among 4-year-olds. Our preschool intervention research had shown us an ever-
widening gap between the high vocabulary growth rates
of the professors' children and the lower vocabulary
growth rates of children from families in poverty; the
gap seemed to foreshadow the findings from school research that in high school many children from families

in poverty lack the vocabulary used in advanced textbooks. Our observations of 42 children learning to talk at home showed us a comparable widening gap at age 3 between the vocabulary growth rates of children in professional families and children in welfare families. But we also saw among the 23 working-class children an average vocabulary growth rate we could use as a basis for considering intervention.

The longitudinal data showed us that the most important difference among families was in the amount of talking that went on. Because the richness of the quality features in utterances addressed to children during everyday parenting varied so little among the families, increased amounts of talking provided some children vastly more experience with nearly every quality feature of language and interaction. We exemplified in logical combinations of the quality features five categories of significant family experience: the Language Diversity contributed by lots of talk; the proportional amounts of encouragement and discouragement contributed by Feedback Tone; Symbolic Emphasis on names, relations, and recall; a Guidance Style focused on asking rather than demanding; and Responsiveness that stressed the importance of the child's behavior during interactions. Experience with these categories in the second and third years of life contributes to breadth of knowledge, analytic and symbolic competencies, self-confidence, and problem solving, which are among the interlocking attitudes, skills, and knowledge required for entry and success in an increasingly technological world of work.

Although these categories of significant family experience certainly do not describe the only aspects of parenting important for competence in society, they may be most important for the language-based analytic and symbolic competencies upon which advanced education and a global economy depend. These competencies may become increasingly important as society separates into technological and service sectors. The longitudinal data showed that differences in the amount of cumulative experience children had with these categories of significant family experience were strongly linked to differences at age 3 in children's rates of vocabulary growth, vocabulary use, and general accomplishments and strongly linked to differences in school performance at age 9.

Is Experience in These Early Years Really That Important?

We learned from the longitudinal data that the problem of skill differences among children at the time of school entry is bigger, more intractable, and more important than we had thought. So much is happening to children during their first 3 years at home, at a time when they are especially malleable and uniquely dependent on the family for virtually all their experience, that by age 3 an intervention must address not just a lack of knowledge or skill, but an entire general approach to experience.

Cognitively, experience is sequential: Experiences in infancy establish habits of seeking, noticing, and incorporating new and more complex experiences, as well as schemas for categorizing and thinking about experiences. Neurologically, infancy is a critical period because cortical development is influenced by the amount of central nervous system activity stimulated by experience. Behaviorally, infancy is a unique time of helplessness when nearly all of children's experience is mediated by adults in one-to-one interactions permeated with affect. Once children become independent and can speak for themselves, they gain access to more opportunities for experience. But the amount and diversity of children's past experience influences which new opportunities for experience they notice and choose.

The children we observed all developed normally; they all learned to walk and talk. At age 3 they were all effective speakers; at age 9–10 they were all performing adequately in third grade. But more than basic skills, effective communication, and common knowledge are needed in order to obtain advanced education and to succeed in professional and technical occupations. Skills and knowledge can be improved or retrained; much more intractable are the differences in confidence and motivation gained from years of practice and encouragement in manipulating a vocabulary of symbols and using them to solve problems.

Heredity and maturation set up traits and trends that can be fertilized or poisoned by experience. But people also get better at those things they see and do more; whatever hereditary traits an individual brings to interactions with the environment, the amount of experience the individual has with symbolic language and problem solving cannot be unimportant. The strength of the relationships revealed by the longitudinal data between the amount of children's expressive and receptive experience and their later accomplishments convinced us that whatever the heredity of less advantaged children, more experience could not be irrelevant or wasted.

Do These Data Really Represent the Lives of Children in America?

Before we extrapolate from the longitudinal data to estimate what intervention would need to provide in order to equalize children's early experience, we must consider the particulars of the population we studied and the methodology we used, and the extent to which they limit the applicability of our findings to other populations and to other hours in children's lives.

Most important to emphasize is that we observed only well-functioning families in the mainstream of American culture; none of the families were dysfunctional, severely stressed, abusive, or addicted. None were independently wealthy. No persons with disabilities were present in any of the homes. Although not all the families owned their homes, they were less transient than may be typical. They were more traditional in their values than may be typical; almost one third regularly went to church. The parents may also be seen as more confident; they felt more comfortable about their parenting and child-rearing practices than may be typical.

The findings from the longitudinal data may be less applicable to families living in deteriorating neighborhoods in inner cities where crime is prevalent, to families with children whose language development is delayed or impaired, to bilingual families, and to families who live in rural poverty such as that experienced by migrant workers. Also, the early experience of children in other cultures is likely to differ, as are the skills needed for success; in Navajo culture, for example, talking a great deal may not be considered socially appropriate. Intergenerational transmission in first-generation immigrant families may (or may not) be quite different from that in mainstream American families.

We feel confident, however, about extrapolating to other hours of the day and to other months and years for these 42 families. First, we saw how stable the amount of talking was in the families over the 2 1/2 years—even as the children learned to talk; new babies were born;

parents took jobs; and the times of observations shifted from mornings to afternoons, evenings, and weekends when both parents and all the siblings were at home. Amount of talk *did* change, but similarly in all the families: Parents talked more and gave more affirmative feedback when their children first started to talk, and then they talked less after the children began to talk a lot. We would expect the amount of talking to have varied similarly within families when occasional illnesses, vacations, and anniversaries occurred. Our impressions that the parents were comfortable and unthreatened by observation also suggest that the interactions we recorded were fairly representative of those that occurred when the observer was not present.

Second, we saw the comparability of our findings to those of others. The average number of parent utterances (278 per hour) reported by Wells (see Chapter 3, endnote 2) was comparable to our average number of parent utterances (341 per hour). Hall, Nagy, and Linn[1] reported an average number of parent words (2,118 per hour) addressed to preschoolers similar to the average number we recorded (1,440 per hour). The average of 20,000 words Wagner[2] reported from a full day of recording children's speech is also similar to our data. Unlike Wells, we found only slight differences in talking across the day; in our data talking was going on 37–42 minutes of each hour between 8 A.M. and 7:30 P.M. in an average family.

All parent–child research is based on the assumption that the data (laboratory or field) reflect what people typically do. In most studies, there are as many reasons that the averages would be higher than reported as that they would be lower. But all researchers caution against extrapolating their findings to people and circumstances they did not include. Our data provide us, however, a first approximation to the absolute magnitude of children's early experience, a basis sufficient for estimating the actual size of the intervention task needed to provide equal experience and, thus, equal opportunities to children living in poverty. We depend on future studies to refine this estimate.

How Much Cumulative Experience Do Children Get?

Because the goal of an intervention would be to equalize children's early experience, we need to estimate the amount of experience children of different SES might bring to an intervention that began at age 4. We base our estimate on the remarkable differences our data showed in the relative amounts of children's early experience: Simply in words heard, the average welfare child was having half as much experience per hour (616 words per hour) as the average working-class child (1,251 words per hour) and less than one third that of the average child in a professional family (2,153 words per hour). These relative differences in amount of experience were so durable over the more than 2 years of observations that they provide the best basis we currently have for estimating children's actual life experience.

A linear extrapolation from the averages in the observational data to a 100-hour week (given a 14-hour waking day) shows the average child in the professional families provided with 215,000 words of language experience, the average child in a working-class family provided with 125,000, and the average child in a welfare family provided with 62,000 words of language experience. In a 5,200-hour year, the amount would be 11 million words for a child in a professional family, 6 million words for a child in a working-class family, and 3 million words for a child in a welfare family. In 4 years of such experience, an average child in a professional family would have accumulated experience with almost 45 million words, an average child in a working-class family would have accumulated experience with 26 million words, and an average child in a welfare family would have accumulated experience with 13 million words. By age 4, the average child in a welfare family might have 13 million fewer words of cumulative experience than the average child in a working-class family. This linear extrapolation is shown in Figure 19.

We can extrapolate similarly the relative differences the data showed in children's hourly experience with parent affirmatives and prohibitions. The average child in a professional family was accumulating 32 affirma-

Language Experience

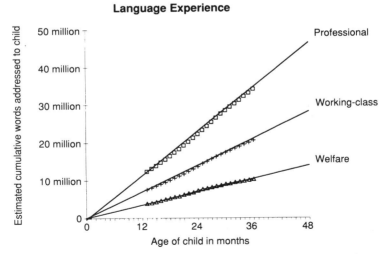

Figure 19.   Estimated cumulative differences in language experience by 4 years of age. (See Appendix B for a detailed explanation of this figure.)

tives and 5 prohibitions per hour, a ratio of 6 encouragements to 1 discouragement. The average child in a working-class family was accumulating 12 affirmatives and 7 prohibitions per hour, a ratio of 2 encouragements to 1 discouragement. The average child in a welfare family, though, was accumulating 5 affirmatives and 11 prohibitions per hour, a ratio of 1 encouragement to 2 discouragements. In a 5,200-hour year, the amount would be 166,000 encouragements to 26,000 discouragements in a professional family, 62,000 encouragements to 36,000 discouragements in a working-class family, and 26,000 encouragements to 57,000 discouragements in a welfare family.

Extrapolated to the first 4 years of life, the average child in a professional family would have accumulated 560,000 more instances of encouraging feedback than discouraging feedback, and an average child in a working-class family would have accumulated 100,000 more encouragements than discouragements. But an average child in a welfare family would have accumulated 125,000 more instances of prohibitions than encouragements. By the age of 4, the average child in a welfare family might have had 144,000 *fewer* encouragements and 84,000 *more* discouragements of his or her behavior than the average child in a working-class family (see Figure 20).

Extrapolating the relative differences in children's hourly experience allows us to estimate children's cumulative experience in the first 4 years of life and so glimpse the size of the problem facing intervention. Whatever the inaccuracy of our estimates, it is not by an order of magnitude such that 60,000 words becomes 6,000 or 600,000. Even if our estimates of children's experience are too high by half, the differences between

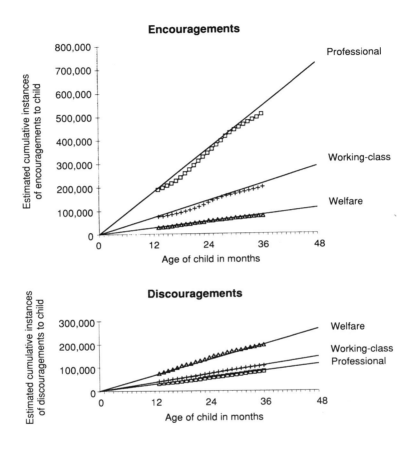

Figure 20. Estimated cumulative differences in confidence-producing experience by 4 years of age. Note the reversal of the lines in the bottom graph, reflecting the prevailing negative Feedback Tone in the welfare homes. (See Appendix B for a detailed explanation of this figure.)

children by age 4 in amounts of cumulative experience are so great that even the best of intervention programs could hope only to keep the welfare children from falling still further behind the children in the working-class families.

How Many Hours of Intervention Are Needed?

Using our extrapolations of the children's average experience in a 100-hour week, we can estimate the hours of intervention needed to keep the experience of the average welfare child equal to that of the average working-class child. We extrapolated to an average welfare child getting experience with 62,000 words per week and to an average working-class child getting experience with 125,000 words per week. To keep the language experience of welfare children equal to that of working-class children, the welfare children would need to receive 63,000 words per week of additional language experience. If the welfare children's home experience gave them 600 words per hour of language experience and an intervention program gave them the 2,100 words per hour average in a professional family, each hour the children were in intervention rather than at home would provide them with a net gain of 1,500 words. Just to provide an average welfare child with an amount of weekly language experience equal to that of an average working-class child would require 41 hours per week of out-of-home experience as rich in words addressed to the child as that in an average professional home.

We extrapolated to an average welfare child accumulating experience with 500 affirmatives and 1,100 prohibitions per week and an average working-class child accumulating experience with 1,200 affirmatives and 700 prohibitions per week. To keep the confidence-building experiences of welfare children equal to those of working-class children, the welfare children would need to be given 1,100 more instances of affirmative feedback per week—700 instances to bring the 500 affirmatives up to the 1,200 given an average working-class child plus 400 affirmatives to reduce the 1,100 prohibitions to the 700 of the average working-class child. It would take 26 hours per week of substituted experience for the average welfare child's experience with affirmatives to equal that of the average working-class child. It would take 66 hours of substituted experience per week to lower the average welfare child's experience with prohibitions to that of the average working-class child. Overall, 40 hours per week of substituted experience would be needed to keep the welfare children's ratio of lifetime experience with encouragement relative to discouragement equal to that of the working-class children.

Any program to provide welfare children with experience equal to that of working-class children would have to start at birth and run continuously all year long. There are no extra hours available to make up for the 60,000 words of experience that may have been lost in some past week. And for caregivers to give 2,100 words of experience every hour to every child in a group setting exceeds the capabilities of even the best of current early childhood programs. Furthermore, such a program would require arranging an environment and organizing activities that would keep young children so engaged that few prohibitions would be called for; such a program would require training staff to be continuously noticing and appreciating children's behavior in order to keep the amount of encouragement high. Even if we have overestimated by half the extra amount of experience the welfare children would need and the effort a program would have to devote each hour to children, it would be difficult to do more than merely keep the welfare children's experience on par with that of the working-class children.

Is It Worth Trying to Change Children's Lives?

Estimating the magnitude of the differences in children's cumulative experience before the age of 3 gives an indication of how big the problem is. Estimating the hours of intervention needed to equalize children's early experience makes clear the enormity of the effort that would be required to change children's lives. And the longer the effort is put off, the less possible the change becomes. We see why our brief, intense efforts during the War on Poverty did not succeed. But we also see the risk to our nation and its children that makes intervention more urgent than ever.

The current trend in American society is toward increasing separation of work in the service sector from analytic, problem-solving work largely restricted to persons with advanced academic training. Since we began this study in 1983, the economic importance of intellectual, symbolic, and problem-solving work has increased and that of blue- and white-collar work has decreased. The social distinctions between the professional and the working class have increased.[3] In our intensive examination of a small sample of American families we saw virtually all the professional families preparing their children for symbolic problem solving from the very beginning of the children's lives. We saw them devoting time and effort to giving their children experience with the language diversity and symbolic emphasis needed for manipulating symbols; we saw them using responsiveness and gentle guidance to encourage problem solving; we saw them providing frequent affirmative feedback to build the confidence and motivation required for sustained independent effort. We saw how strongly related the amount of such experience was to the accomplishments of children from working-class families. But we saw only one third of the working-class families and none of the welfare families similarly preparing their children.[4]

The nearly uniform advantages received by the children of the college-educated professionals suggest the evolution of an increasingly distinct subculture in American society, one in which adults routinely transmit to their offspring the symbolic thinking and confident problem solving that mark the adults' economic activities and that are so difficult for outsiders to acquire in midlife. A trend toward separation into subcultures jeopardizes the upward mobility that has given this nation greatness and presages the tragedy of downward mobility that produces increasing numbers of working poor.

If this trend is to be reversed, a beginning must be made now. The issue is no longer one of eradicating poverty or of putting welfare recipients to work but of reversing a trend, the downward drift of the working class. Given the national commitment to providing equal opportunities to all citizens, as evidenced by support of programs such as Head Start and WIC, it is not a question of whether to intervene but of how to intervene.

Having estimated the amount of experience children would need, we can consider what alternatives there are for intervention, what they would cost, and how long it would take to counteract the threat posed by successive generations of children with ever-fewer skills and less experience to transmit to the next generation. We can ask whether it is possible to actually change children's lives within a single generation if whatever resources were required were committed fully. We can ask whether, if present efforts were expanded, the gains would be sufficient over time to stem the downward drift of the working class and, if not, whether there are any other alternatives worth trying.

Is It Possible to Change Children's Lives in a Generation?

From our extrapolations we estimated the amount of experience an early education program would need to provide to children. To ensure that an average welfare child had a weekly amount of experience equal that of the average child in a working-class family, merely in terms of hours of language experience of any kind (words heard), 41 hours per week of out-of-home experience as rich in words addressed to the child as that in an average professional home would be required. For the ratio of encouragement to total feedback to equal that experienced by the average working-class child, 40 hours per week of substituted experience would be required. Thus, welfare children would need to be in substitute care 40 hours every week from birth onward.

We as a nation could deliver the necessary time and experience for every child who needs it, not just for children in welfare families. We have an example of an intervention program that did this by applying a range of the sophisticated technologies that have been designed to serve people with special needs. As a nation we routinely provide help to families in crisis, enroll children with disabilities in infant stimulation and remediation programs, intervene with dysfunctional families, arrange job training for parents, and deliver quality child care. To provide children the necessary amounts of experience would only require integrating and applying technologies we already have.

205

The Milwaukee Project[5] was an early intervention program that worked. Infants whose mothers' IQ tested as 75 or below were enrolled at 6–8 weeks of age in out-of-home, full-day child care. The transition from the home to full-day child care was made by having the paraprofessional who would become the infant's individual caregiver spend 3–5 hours, 3 days a week, in the family home with the mother, participating in family activities, talking about the mother's concerns, and advising her about parenting and environmental arrangements. When the infant entered full-day child care, the mother entered a program combining remedial education classes and on-the-job training as a nurse's aide guided by an experienced employee. The children in the Milwaukee Project, unlike children from comparable families not enrolled in the project and unlike children in other less time-consuming intervention programs, were equal to the national average in accomplishments at age 8.

The comprehensive program of the Milwaukee Project included many components that have become fairly standard in programs such as WIC and Parents as Teachers (PAT)[6] that serve low-income families: parent education and training classes, parent group meetings, resource centers, and a welfare-to-work program. The Milwaukee Project used parent coaching, which is the technology that family preservation programs such as Homebuilders[7] have used successfully to improve the daily lives of entire families. Parent coaching provides a coach who works in the home one-to-one with a parent to find out what changes are needed to improve daily interactions in the home and to help the parent incorporate these changes into the parent's individual lifestyle. The coach remains in the home as long as needed and gives as much support and advice as needed to help the parent arrange a home environment and activity schedule conducive to improvements in interactions and child care.

Parent coaching becomes job coaching at the place of paid employment. The coach provides one-to-one, on-the-job coaching for people who need help to sell themselves during an initial interview, to perform a particular task, or to decide how to dress and what to say or ask for and when. As in the home, the coach is there to model, guide, and help an individual as long as needed. An employer may have to help pay the coach but is assured that the job gets done and meets standards for quality. Welfare-to-work programs use job coaching to provide parents with skills, a paycheck, and the dignity of work; the programs also serve to undo the detrimental effects of isolation by getting welfare parents participating on a regular basis in the lives of middle-class people.

Quality out-of-home care can be provided for infants and young children, even though it so rarely is. The kinds of learning experiences and nurturing that developing children need have been well documented, as have the arrangements needed to provide environments that are safer and more stimulating than most homes.[8] Procedures to get and keep children engaged in learning activities, to provide physical exercise and adequate nutrition, and to teach self-care skills have been described in detail; as have procedures for training, supervising, and monitoring staff interactions with children. The technology is available that could actually provide welfare children with the amount of language and interaction, the 2,100 words and 32 affirmatives per hour, we estimated that children in professional families experience per week.

The Milwaukee Project showed that a comprehensive program, beginning at birth and integrating all the

207

technology routinely available to families in crisis and children with special needs, is within this nation's capabilities. It is possible to provide all children equal experience and thus equal opportunity. But to implement even a small local program serving 17 families in Milwaukee required the enthusiasm of the War on Poverty, resolute reallocation of resources, and some sacrifice of American values about the sanctity and responsibilities of families.

It is possible to change children's lives within a generation, but the cost would be immense. To organize, implement, and monitor on a nationwide scale an intervention as intensive as the Milwaukee Project would require far more in money, efficiency, and accountability than has so far been achieved in the limited intervention known as Head Start. Even more difficult might be enlisting the support of families who are struggling themselves and persuading them to undertake the sacrifices necessary to provide a better future for other people's children.

Why Not Just Do More of What Is Being Done Now?

Inertia, divided opinion, and uncertainty about outcomes virtually assure that what is being done now will continue to be done—a bit of prevention and a lot of repair. Established programs will continue to provide nutrition through WIC, help to families in crisis, foster care to neglected children, training and counseling to parents, services to children with special needs, remedial classes in public schools, and retraining as industrial jobs are lost. Head Start will be continued and extended to a larger number of children and to younger children.

Early intervention programs that provide enriched experience *do* improve the lives of children. A long-term follow-up study undertaken when children from 11 different early intervention programs were 8–18 years old showed that in public school fewer of these children had been retained in grade or placed in special education classes, more had stayed in school, and more had been employed after graduation.[9] Over successive generations, these children's increased experience will be transmitted to their children, who will add still more experience through the continuation of existing early intervention programs, especially those that follow through into elementary school.

Present intervention programs are familiar; their cost and relative effectiveness are known. There are questions, though, concerning their long-term effectiveness. Intergenerational transmission of enriched experience takes years, and whether this process will keep pace with the increasing demands of a technological society and the growing numbers of families raising children in poverty remains uncertain. Employers already need to include remedial language classes as part of job training and to hire foreign nationals for work in science and engineering. Declining competitiveness with other nations has become a national concern; it is increasingly unclear whether present intervention programs are commensurate with the complexity of the problem they were designed to help solve.

Is Parenting the Problem?

Intergenerational transmission of a culture and its knowledge passes from parent to child. During the first years of life when almost everything a child learns depends on what the family provides, parenting puts in place not only fundamental skills and understandings but also an entire general approach to experience. Our data showed that the magnitude of children's accomplishments depends less on the material and educational advantages available in the home and more on the amount of experience children accumulate with parenting that provides language diversity, affirmative feedback, symbolic emphasis, gentle guidance, and responsiveness. By the time children are 3 years old, even intensive intervention cannot make up for the differences in the amount of such experience children have received from their parents. If children could be given better parenting, intervention might be unnecessary.

Our observations showed us, though, how hard American parents are trying now to provide better futures for their children. All the parents we observed wanted their children to be successful students and productive citizens. Many sought advice and read books on how to be better parents. Working-class families were seen to be following the route traditional in an economic system that for generations produced upward mobility: Mothers took jobs so the family could move to a newer house and a better school system in the suburbs. Families went into debt to secure an environment for their children in which parents did not need to prohibit exploration in order to keep their children safe, an environment in which their children would be casually introduced to the next rung up, the skills and values of their better-educated neighbors.

Among the working-class parents, the choice to be consumers and to make the financial commitment necessary to move to the suburbs promised both immediate and future advantages for their children. But those advantages required a second income, and most of that went to pay for child care. Parents wanted enriched experience for their children but could not find it, could not get to it, or could not afford it. We wondered why any of the parents chose to stay at home and make do with less in an effort to become better parents. Yet one third of the working-class parents chose to sacrifice material advantages in order to spend time providing their children with the enriched experience that would prepare them for advanced skill training or higher education.[10]

The difficulties of parenting encourage the choice to be consumers. Even among the highly educated parents with extensive skills in gentle guidance, we saw the challenges parents face daily in persuading children to participate in reading a story rather than watching a video, to undertake chores such as picking up their many toys, to eat healthy foods, and to refrain from exploring dangerous equipment and fragile possessions. Parenting in a society without television, toy stores, gas-powered lawn mowers, and sugar-coated cereals was easier by far. Technology has removed parents' need for children's help, the traditional means by which parents transmitted across generations the importance of work, and has left parents to guide their children as best they can through a maze of continuously available entertainment.

At the same time that parenting has become a dauntingly demanding job, the competencies needed to prepare for and to participate in an increasingly technological world of work have multiplied. Parents with little experience or knowledge concerning such competencies have always depended on teachers and schooling to provide them to their children. Yet the cumulative experience of many children is such that the most the public schools can do is to prepare the children for unskilled jobs that no longer exist. There can be scant hope for better parenting in a society that assumes that nuclear families and single-parent households can turn out well-informed, highly motivated, and well-behaved children in conditions that would almost certainly lead any other enterprise into bankruptcy. Entrusting the future of the nation and the lives of its children to a work force of parents offered little training, no support, and no quality control can continue only if there is no alternative.

Is There an Alternative?

Helping parents is an alternative worth trying. Rather than design or expand early intervention programs, this country could focus on helping parents ensure that their children get enough early experience so that differences never become so great as to be intractable to even the most effective intervention. The nation could commit to a goal of ensuring that all children get enriched experience and models of good parenting whether at home or in child care facilities. It would not be possible to ensure that all children would match the accomplishments of advantaged children, but it would be feasible to make them better parents and thus improve intergenerational transmission over the long term.

Parents could be helped by making quality child care affordable for all parents on an income-graded basis. Children would receive experience with good parenting and planned developmental activities; parents would see models and get feedback and informal advice about child rearing. Quality child care would provide, from infancy, whatever additional hours of language and affirmative feedback children might need. All working parents would benefit from what only a few can now afford: the support that quality child care provides, which enables parents to be productive on the job rather than worried about their children. Creating neighborhood child care centers could provide part-day enriched experience to children and a locus for early diagnostic and intervention services, a haven for families in crisis, and a training site for parents of children at risk.[11]

Parents could be helped by making parent aides available, the extra pair of hands that extended family once provided. Especially for young people, working as parent aides would provide experience with how well-functioning families work together, the amount of talking and kinds of experience they provide their children, the environments they arrange, and the expectations they hold. A program of parent aides would provide apprenticeships in good parenting.

Parents could be helped by making mentors available to all parents. A mentor would provide one-to-one parent coaching if needed, but in most cases the mentor would be a friendly, more knowledgeable and experienced person chosen by a parent to visit the home and to watch, listen, and talk with the parent. Mentors in the past were members of the community of extended family who transmitted knowledge about societal standards and developmental expectations for child behavior; about strategies for coping with, or preventing, misbehavior; and about the possible consequences, good or bad, of what parents were doing with their children from moment to moment.

Parents could be helped by the establishment of a national policy that is as concerned with children's early experience as it is with their health and nutrition. A national commitment to support good parenting could encourage mothers who enjoyed interacting with children

213

to stay at home and provide mothers who wanted to work with choices concerning the amount and quality of the experience their children were getting outside the home. The need for helping parents, through subsidies or family allowances, has been publicly stated for years; other countries have shown the feasibility of this alternative and its benefits to families and children.

Why Is Deciding to Help Parents So Difficult?

Paying for subsidies, and using tax revenues for that purpose, cannot be the real issue when subsidizing parenting is considered. The nation routinely pays for cropland left fallow, guarantees mortgages and deposits in savings and loan institutions, and provides tax abatements to businesses. Neither can the threat of socialism be an issue in a country that provides unemployment benefits, Medicare, and Social Security. Nor can the form of government be an issue when Americans consider what the alternative system in the Yugoslavia of yesterday accomplished relative to the intergenerational transmission of culture.

In America the culture we see in intergenerational transmission is the democracy de Tocqueville described in 1835.[12] Americans can recognize themselves still as a resolutely individualistic people, categorically committed to the profit motive. Looking beyond stated beliefs to visible benefits, it is apparent that healthy people will pay for Medicaid because they might need it themselves someday. People will pay for universal education because they benefit from getting children off the streets and out of the unskilled labor market. But childless people will resist paying for services they will never use. Parents will defend their right to do as they please with

214

their children, and everyone will draw the line at invading the privacy of the home.

In a democracy the will of the majority may determine election outcomes, but the priorities of the people are communicated through lobbies and special interest groups. Almost anyone can form a special interest group to advocate for particular rights and to ensure profits. The Farm Bureau speaks out in favor of school lunches and the distribution of free commodities because farmers benefit. Advocating for children's rights can profit a law firm just as a special interest in studying parent–child interactions can benefit an academic career. A first step toward subsidies for good parenting may have been taken by the well-educated advocates of extended parental leave programs and flexible work hours.

Working-class parents, like the assembly-line workers in the early auto industry, await the leaders who will educate them about where their interests lie and what potential profits would accrue from forming a special interest group. With the loss of industrial jobs and the increasing separation of work in the service sector from analytic problem-solving work, the upward mobility of working-class families will increasingly depend on preparing their children for advanced skill training or higher education. To ensure a better life for their children, working-class parents will have to add to their traditional duties a concern with giving their children early experience with many of the competencies they had always depended on schooling to provide.

As working-class parents are made aware that the amount of experience provided to children in advantaged families could be provided to their children, by themselves if they could afford to stay at home, or by someone else if they could afford to enroll their children in quality care outside the home, they will organize a special interest group whose issue is the need for help with the immense responsibilities a technological society has so casually assigned them. A special interest group of working-class parents will join with other special interest groups representing families, educators, and child care and social service providers to lobby for helping parents. Joining them might then be a national commitment to providing a voice to those who cannot form a special interest group to demand equal cumulative experience, the infants and toddlers upon whom the nation's future depends.

Endnotes

1. Hall, Nagy, and Linn (1984) audiorecorded 5 hours (2 1/2 hours on 2 consecutive days) of parents talking to their children at home and during walks to preschool and talk with and by the children's teachers at preschool. The children were 4 1/2–5 years old; 19 (10 African American) were working-class children and 20 (11 African American) were middle-class children. The middle-class adults averaged 2,383 words per hour; their children averaged 1,713. The working-class adults averaged 1,840 words per hour; their children averaged 1,455.

2. Wagner (1985) reported speech data, standardized to a 12-hour waking day, from 12 studies of children 1 1/2–14 years of age. The children said about 20,000 words in 1 day and used about 3,000 different words. Children age 3 1/2 said about 100 words per minute. Wagner also discussed some important considerations concerning the recording of spontaneous speech, such as how representative it is of speech when children are not being recorded.

3. Reich (1991) described this trend; he linked it to the shift from a national to a global economy and cited the reasons that it will accelerate.

4. All the professional families were above average on four or more of the five categories of significant family experience. Their parenting reflects the diversity of vocabulary and Symbolic Emphasis in their speech to their children, the problem-solving style of their guidance, and their willingness to respond to their children's initiatives and to give encouraging feedback. Only 8 of the working-class families (5 of the 10 white-collar, 3 of the 13 blue-collar) and none of the welfare families showed this pattern.

5. See Garber (1988) for a complete description of the Milwaukee Project's design and results.

6. Participation in WIC (see Chapter 2, endnote 10), the nutritional program for low income families, requires attendance at parent meetings. Parents as Teachers (PAT) is a program for parents with children from birth to 3 years of age that includes group meetings and home visits; among its goals are realistic expectations for child behavior and methods of positive discipline.
7. Homebuilders is perhaps the most well-known of state-funded family preservation programs. (Homebuilders is based at the Behavioral Sciences Institute, 34004 Ninth Avenue South, Suite 8, Federal Way, Washington 98003.) Family preservation programs are brief, intense interventions for families who are about to lose their children. For 4–5 weeks the family has 24-hour access to individually tailored, goal-oriented services, all delivered within the home and community.
8. The Infant Center (Herbert-Jackson et al., 1977) and Toddler Center (O'Brien, Porterfield, Herbert-Jackson, & Risley, 1979) were fully operational programs of all-day out-of-home care that were also documented demonstrations of optimum child care procedures.
9. See Lazar and Darlington (1982) for a report of the findings of the Consortium for Longitudinal Studies, which undertook a monumental reanalysis of the raw data from 11 very different early intervention programs, an undertaking as awesome to read about as the Bristol study. (See Chapter 3, endnote 2.)
10. If you are a working parent reading this and wondering about your choice to go to work, we note that the data do not suggest that you need to stay at home with your child. The remarkable consistency of the parenting we observed suggests that if you are concerned about whether you are doing your best for your child, you are probably among those parents above average on most of the parenting variables. Your thoughts should rather be about the time your child does *not* spend with you. The data show that the most important consideration is the

amount of cumulative experience your child has with language and interaction; anyone, educated or not, who enjoys talking with children can deliver this necessary time and attention. The more time your child spends in the care of other people, the more carefully you need to choose caregivers and the more attentively you need to monitor the amount of experience with language and interaction your child is actually receiving while in alternative care.

11. The organization of child care and recreation centers and of parent advice and mentoring programs, and the methods for efficient mastery training of the people who work in them, were described as early as 1976 by Risley, Clark, and Cataldo (1976).

12. DeTocqueville (1835) was a French aristocrat who spent 9 months in America in 1831–1832 examining the nature and workings of American democracy to see how it might be applied in Europe following the French Revolution. Reading his account, it is amazing to see how little Americans seem to have changed in 150 years.

References
◆◆◆◆

Barker, R.G., & Wright, H.F. (1951). *One boy's day. A specimen record of behavior.* New York: Harper & Row.

Baumrind, D. (1971). Current patterns of parental authority. *Developmental Psychology Monographs, 4,* 99–103.

Bayley, N., & Schaefer, E.S. (1964). Correlations of maternal and child behaviors with the development of mental abilities: Data from the Berkeley Growth Study. *Monographs of the Society for Research in Child Development, 29* (6, Serial No. 97).

Becker, W.C. (1977). Teaching reading and language to the disadvantaged: What we have learned from field research. *Harvard Educational Review, 47,* 518–543.

Belsky, J., Gilstrap, B., & Rovine, M. (1984). The Pennsylvania Infant and Family Development Project, I: Stability and change in mother–infant and father–infant interaction in a family setting at one, three, and nine months. *Child Development, 55,* 692–705.

Bereiter, C., & Englemann, S. (1966). *Teaching disadvantaged children in the preschool.* Englewood Cliffs, NJ: Prentice Hall.

Bernstein, B. (1970). A sociolinguistic approach to socialization: With some reference to educability. In F. Williams (Ed.), *Language and poverty: Perspectives on a theme* (pp. 25–61). Chicago: Markham Publishing.

Bloom, L. (1993). *The transition from infancy to language: Acquiring the power of expression.* New York: Cambridge University Press.

Bloom, L., Rocissano, L., & Hood, L. (1976). Adult–child discourse: Developmental interaction between information processing and linguistic knowledge. *Cognitive Psychology, 8,* 521–552.

Bretherton, I., & Waters, E. (1985). Growing points of attachment theory and research. *Monographs of the Society for Research in Child Development, 50* (1–2, Serial No. 209).

Brottman, M.A. (Ed.). (1968). Language remediation for the disadvantaged child. *Monographs of the Society for Research in Child Development, 33* (8, Serial No. 124).

Brown, R. (1973). *A first language: The early stages.* Cambridge, MA: Harvard University Press.

Brown, P., & Levinson, S. (1978). Universals in language usage: Politeness phenomena. In E.N. Goody (Ed.), *Questions and politeness: Strategies in social interaction* (pp. 56–289). New York: Cambridge University Press.

Capaldi, D., & Patterson, G.R. (1987). An approach to the problem of recruitment and retention rates for longitudinal research. *Behavioral Assessment, 9,* 169–177.

221

Carmichael, L. (Ed.). (1954). *Manual of child psychology*. New York: John Wiley & Sons.

Chase-Lansdale, P.L., Mott, F. L., Brooks-Gunn, J., & Phillips, D.A. (1991). Children of the National Longitudinal Survey of Youth: A unique research opportunity. *Developmental Psychology, 27,* 918–931.

CTBS. (1987). *Comprehensive Tests of Basic Skills* (CTBS/U, 3rd ed.). Monterey, CA: CTB/McGraw-Hill.

deTocqueville, A. (1945). *Democracy in America.* (H. Reeve, Trans.). New York: Alfred A. Knopf. (Original work published 1835.)

Deutsch, M. (1967). *The disadvantaged child.* New York: Basic Books.

Dunn, L.M. (1965). *Peabody Picture Vocabulary Test.* Circle Pines, MN: American Guidance Service.

Dunn, L.W., & Dunn, L.M. (1981). *Peabody Picture Vocabulary Test–Revised* (Forms L and M). Circle Pines, MN: American Guidance Service.

Durkin, K. (1987). Minds and language: Social cognition, social interaction, and the acquisition of language. *Mind and Language, 2,* 105–140.

Fletcher, P., & Garman, M. (Eds.). (1986). *Language acquisition: Studies in first language development.* New York: Cambridge University Press.

Furstenberg, F.F., Jr. (1985). Sociological ventures in child development. *Child Development, 56,* 281–288.

Garber, H.L. (1988). *The Milwaukee Project: Preventing mental retardation in children at risk.* Washington, DC: American Association on Mental Retardation.

Gazaway, R. (1969). *The longest mile.* Garden City, NY: Doubleday.

Gleason, J.B. (1985). Language and socialization. In F.S. Kessel (Ed.), *The development of language and language researchers: Essays in honor of Roger Brown* (pp. 269–280). Hillsdale, NJ: Lawrence Erlbaum Associates.

Goody, E. N. (1978). Towards a theory of questions. In E.N. Goody (Ed.), *Questions and politeness: Strategies in social interaction* (pp. 17–43). New York: Cambridge University Press.

Gottfried, A.W. (Ed.). (1984). *Home environment and early cognitive development: Longitudinal research.* New York: Academic Press.

Gray, S.W., & Klaus, R.A. (1968). The Early Training Project and its general rationale. In R.D. Hess & R.M. Baer (Eds.), *Early education* (pp. 63–70). Chicago: Aldine.

Hall, W.S., Nagy, W.E., & Linn, R. (1984). *Spoken words: Effects of situation and social group on oral word usage and frequency.* Hillsdale, NJ: Lawrence Erlbaum Associates.

Hammill, D.D., & Newcomer, P.L. (1988). *Test of Language Development–2: Intermediate.* Austin, TX: PRO-ED.

Harris, M. (1993). *Language experience and early language development: From input to uptake.* Hillsdale, NJ: Lawrence Erlbaum Associates.

Hart, B. (1982). Process in the teaching of pragmatics. In L. Feagans & D. Farran (Eds.), *The language of children reared in poverty* (pp. 199–218). San Diego: Academic Press.

Hart, B. (1983). Assessing spontaneous speech. *Behavioral Assessment, 5,* 71–82.

Hart, B., & Risley, T.R. (1975). Incidental teaching of language in the preschool. *Journal of Applied Behavior Analysis, 8,* 411–420.

Hart, B., & Risley, T.R. (1978). Promoting productive language through incidental teaching. *Education in Urban Society, 10,* 407–429.

Hart, B., & Risley, T.R. (1980). *In vivo* language intervention: Unanticipated general effects. *Journal of Applied Behavior Analysis, 12,* 407–432.

Hart, B., & Risley, T.R. (1981). Grammatical and conceptual growth in the language of psychosocially disadvantaged children: Assessment and intervention. In M.J. Begab, H.C. Haywood, & H.L. Garber (Eds.), *Psychosocial influences in retarded performance: Vol. 2. Strategies for improving competence* (pp. 181–198). Baltimore: University Park Press.

Hart, B., & Risley, T.R. (1982). *How to use incidental teaching.* Austin, TX: PRO-ED.

Hart, B., & Risley, T.R. (1989). The longitudinal study of interactive systems. *Education and Treatment of Children, 12,* 347–358.

Hart, B., & Risley, T.R. (1992). American parenting of language-learning children: Persisting differences in family–child interactions observed in natural home environments. *Developmental Psychology, 28,* 1096–1105.

Heath, S.B. (1983). *Ways with words: Language, life, and work in communities and classrooms.* New York: Cambridge University Press.

Herbert-Jackson, E., O'Brien, M., Porterfield, J., & Risley, T.R. (1977). *The infant center: A complete guide to organizing and managing infant day care.* Baltimore: University Park Press.

Huston, A.C. (Ed.). (1991). *Children in poverty: Child development and public policy.* New York: Cambridge University Press.

Huston, A.C., Wright, J.C., Rice, M.L., Kerkman, D., & St. Peters, M. (1990). Development of television viewing patterns in early childhood: A longitudinal investigation. *Developmental Psychology, 26,* 409–420.

Jastak, S., & Wilkinson, G.S. (1984). *The Wide Range Achievement Test–Revised.* Wilmington, DE: Jastak Associates, Inc.

Karnes, M.B., Hodgins, A.S., Stoneburner, R.L., Studley, W.M., & Teska, J.A. (1968). Effects of a highly structured program of language development on intellectual functioning and psycholinguistic development of culturally disadvantaged three-year-olds. *Journal of Special Education, 2,* 405–412.

Lazar, I., & Darlington, R. (1982). Lasting effects of early education: A report from the Consortium for Longitudinal Studies. *Monographs of the Society for Research in Child Development, 47* (2–3, Serial No. 195).

Maccoby, E.E., & Martin, J.A. (1983). Socialization in the context of the family: Parent–child interaction. In E. M. Hetherington (Ed.), *Handbook of child psychology: Vol. 4. Socialization, personality, and social development* (pp. 1–101). New York: John Wiley & Sons.

McFarlane, M. (1994). *Nonlinear multilevel modeling of growth.* Unpublished doctoral dissertation, University of North Carolina at Chapel Hill.

Mead, M. (1928). *Coming of age in Samoa.* New York: Morrow.

Menard, N., & Santerre, L. (1979). La richesse lexicale individuelle comme marquer sociolinguistique [Individual lexical richness as a sociolinguistic marker]. *Cahier de Linguistique, 9,* 165–190.

Moerk, E.L. (1992). *A first language taught and learned.* Baltimore: Paul H. Brookes Publishing Co.

Montessori, M. (1912). *The Montessori method.* New York: F.A. Stokes.

Nelson, K. (1986). Event knowledge and cognitive development. In K. Nelson (Ed.), *Event knowledge* (pp. 231–247). Hillsdale, NJ: Lawrence Erlbaum Associates.

O'Brien, M.O., Porterfield, J., Herbert-Jackson, E., & Risley, T.R. (1979). *The toddler center: A practical guide to day care for one- and two-year olds.* Baltimore: University Park Press.

Otis, A.S., & Lennon, R.T. (1989). *Otis-Lennon School Ability Test* (6th ed., OLSAT). San Antonio, TX: The Psychological Corporation.

Patterson, G.R., DeBaryshe, B.D., & Ramsey, E. (1989). A developmental perspective on antisocial behavior. *American Psychologist, 44,* 329–335.

Reich, R.B. (1991). *The work of nations: Preparing ourselves for 21st century capitalism.* New York: Alfred A. Knopf.

Rice, M.L., & Kemper, S. (1984). *Child language and cognition: Contemporary issues.* Baltimore: University Park Press.

Richman, A.L., LeVine, R.A., New, R.S., Howrigan, G.A., Welles-Nystrom, B., & LeVine, S.E. (1988, Summer). Maternal behavior to infants in five cultures. In R.A. LeVine, P.M. Miller, & M.M. West

(Eds.), *Parental behavior in diverse societies. New directions for child development, No. 40* (pp. 81–96). San Francisco: Jossey-Bass.

Risley, T.R. (1977a). The development and maintenance of language: An operant model. In B.C. Etzel, J.M. LeBlanc, & D.M. Baer (Eds.), *New developments in behavioral research: Theory, method, and application. In honor of Sidney W. Bijou* (pp. 81–101). Hillsdale, NJ: Lawrence Erlbaum Associates.

Risley, T.R. (1977b). The ecology of applied behavior analysis. In A. Rogers-Warren & S.F. Warren (Eds.), *Ecological perspectives in behavior analysis* (pp. 149–163). Baltimore: University Park Press.

Risley, T.R., Clark, H.B., & Cataldo, M.F. (1976). Behavioral technology for the normal middle-class family. In E.J. Mash, L.C. Handy, & L.A. Hamerlynck (Eds.), *Behavior modification and families* (pp. 34–60). New York: Brunner/Mazel.

Risley, T.R., Hart, B., & Doke, L.A. (1971). Operant language development: The outline of a therapeutic technology. In R.L. Schiefelbusch (Ed.), *Language of the mentally retarded* (pp. 107–123). Baltimore: University Park Press.

Risley, T.R., & Reynolds, N. (1970). Emphasis as a prompt for verbal imitation. *Journal of Applied Behavior Analysis, 3,* 185–190.

Schieffelin, B.B., & Ochs, E. (1978). A cultural perspective on the transition from prelinguistic to linguistic communication. In R.M. Golinkoff (Ed.), *The transition from prelinguistic to linguistic communication* (pp. 115–131). Hillsdale, NJ: Lawrence Erlbaum Associates.

Schumaker, J.B., & Sherman, J.A. (1978). Parent as intervention agent from birth onward. In R.L. Schiefelbusch (Ed.), *Language intervention strategies* (pp. 237–315). Baltimore: University Park Press.

Smith, M.D., & Locke, J.L. (Eds.). (1988). *The emergent lexicon: The child's development of a linguistic vocabulary.* New York: Academic Press.

Snow, C.E. (1986). Conversations with children. In P. Fletcher & M. Garman (Eds.), *Language acquisition: Studies in first language development* (pp. 69–89). New York: Cambridge University Press.

SPSS Inc. (1988). SPSS/PC+™. Chicago: Author.

Stanley, J.C. (Ed.). (1972). *Preschool programs for the disadvantaged: Five experimental approaches to early childhood education.* Baltimore: Johns Hopkins University Press.

Stevens, G., & Cho, J.H. (1985). Socioeconomic indexes and the 1980 census occupational classification scheme. *Social Science Research, 14,* 142–168.

Terman, L.M., & Merrill, M.A. (1960). *Stanford-Binet Intelligence Scale: Manual for the Third Revision Form L-M.* Boston: Houghton Mifflin.

Thissen, D., & Bock, R.D. (1990). Linear and nonlinear curve fitting. In A. von Eye (Ed.), *Statistical methods in longitudinal research: Vol. II. Time series and categorical longitudinal data* (pp. 289–318). San Diego: Academic Press.

Vygotsky, L.S. (1978). *Mind in society.* Cambridge, MA: Harvard University Press.

Wagner, K.R. (1985). How much do children say in a day? *Journal of Child Language, 12,* 475–487.

Walden, T.A. (1993). Communicating the meaning of events through social referencing. In A.P. Kaiser & D.B. Gray (Eds.), *Communication and language intervention series: Vol. 2. Enhancing children's communication: Research foundations for intervention* (pp. 187–199). Baltimore: Paul H. Brookes Publishing Co.

Walker, D., Greenwood, C., Hart, B., & Carta, J. (1994). Prediction of school outcomes based on early language production and socioeconomic factors. *Child Development, 65,* 606–621.

Weikart, D.P. (1972). Relationship of curriculum, teaching, and learning in preschool education. In J.C. Stanley (Ed.), *Preschool programs for the disadvantaged: Five experimental approaches to early childhood education* (pp. 22–66). Baltimore: Johns Hopkins University Press.

Weikart, D.P., Bond, J.T., & McNeil, J.T. (1978). The Ypsilanti Perry Preschool Project: Preschool years and longitudinal results. *Monographs of the High/Scope Educational Research Foundation,* No. 3.

Weinberg, A. (1989). Intelligence and IQ. *American Psychologist, 44,* 98–104.

Wells, G. (1985). *Language development in the preschool years.* New York: Cambridge University Press.

Wells, G. (1986). Variations in child language. In P. Fletcher & M. Garman (Eds.), *Language acquisition: Studies in first language development* (pp. 109–139). New York: Cambridge University Press.

White, B.L. (1985). *Experience and environment. Vol. 2.* Englewood Cliffs, NJ: Prentice Hall.

Whiting, J.W.M., & Whiting, B. B. (1978). *Children of six cultures: A psychocultural analysis.* Cambridge, MA: Harvard University Press.

Zaslow, M., & Rogoff, B. (1981). The cross-cultural study of early interaction: Implications from research in culture and cognition. In T. Field, A. Sostek, P. Vietze, & H. Leiderman (Eds.), *Culture and early interactions* (pp. 237–256). Hillsdale, NJ: Lawrence Erlbaum Associates.

Appendix A
Quality Features

◆ ◆ ◆ ◆

Quality features of parent language and interaction averaged when children were 13–36 months old

Rank	SEI	Amount per hour: Language — Vocabulary (Different)						Amount per hour: Language — All words					Amount per hour: Language — Sentences (Verb tenses)			Amount per hour: Interaction — Discourse functions			Amount per hour: Interaction — Questions			Amount per hour: Interaction — Adjacency conditions			Amount per hour: Interaction — Valence		Richness per utterance: Language — Vocabulary (All words)					Richness per utterance: Language — Sentences (Verb tenses)			Richness per utterance: Interaction — Discourse functions			Richness per utterance: Interaction — Questions			Richness per utterance: Interaction — Adjacency conditions			Richness per utterance: Interaction — Valence	
		Utterances	Words	Nouns	Verbs	Modifiers	Functors	Words	Nouns	Verbs	Modifiers	Functors	2+clause	Past	Future	Declaratives	Imperatives	All	Wh	Y/n	Aux-fronted	Initiate	Respond	Floorhold	Affirm	Prohibit	Words	Nouns	Verbs	Modifiers	Functors	2+clause	Past	Future	Declaratives	Imperatives	All	Wh	Y/n	Aux-fronted	Initiate	Respond	Floorhold	Affirm	Prohibit
1	88.28	335	337	89	120	45	83	1495	182	406	112	737	42	33	13	109	32	102	45	56	34	25	142	172	14	4	4.33	.51	1.18	.32	2.16	.12	.09	.04	.31	.10	.31	.13	.17	.10	.08	.44	.51	.05	.01
2	82.48	404	423	117	155	55	97	2134	216	599	156	1119	70	33	24	185	25	113	56	56	28	37	207	166	40	3	5.36	.52	1.52	.40	2.81	.18	.08	.06	.46	.06	.28	.13	.15	.07	.09	.53	.42	.10	.01
3	82.48	374	284	74	105	29	76	1422	158	415	77	723	28	19	16	103	52	112	51	61	31	41	162	182	27	3	3.83	.42	1.12	.21	1.95	.07	.05	.05	.27	.14	.30	.13	.16	.08	.12	.45	.49	.07	.01
4	81.61	549	423	113	158	53	99	2635	256	755	178	1349	94	43	20	186	55	195	86	109	59	34	289	231	47	5	4.73	.46	1.37	.31	2.43	.17	.08	.04	.33	.10	.36	.16	.20	.11	.07	.52	.42	.08	.01
5	79.72	508	408	116	153	45	94	2310	292	685	119	1148	68	35	24	173	56	155	52	102	59	46	199	273	23	1	4.48	.56	1.33	.23	2.22	.13	.07	.05	.33	.11	.30	.10	.20	.12	.10	.39	.54	.04	.00
6	79.63	692	460	123	180	54	102	2845	311	821	142	1406	86	63	26	190	152	175	111	64	21	20	353	334	46	10	4.10	.45	1.19	.21	2.05	.12	.09	.04	.27	.22	.25	.16	.09	.03	.03	.52	.48	.07	.01
7	78.97	732	469	132	183	53	100	3504	453	1045	173	1754	104	52	54	323	86	172	49	122	60	24	297	423	29	5	4.78	.62	1.43	.23	2.40	.14	.07	.07	.44	.12	.23	.07	.17	.08	.03	.41	.58	.04	.01
8	76.87	578	403	132	141	43	88	2501	361	655	136	1264	53	34	25	226	67	112	29	83	41	51	211	309	37	3	4.57	.65	1.20	.25	2.32	.10	.06	.05	.41	.12	.21	.05	.15	.07	.09	.40	.56	.07	.01
9	66.03	243	260	69	93	26	72	1019	139	290	51	507	25	21	10	80	35	60	24	36	16	21	102	124	17	2	4.29	.55	1.21	.21	2.18	.11	.08	.05	.32	.15	.26	.11	.15	.07	.09	.45	.51	.07	.01
10	64.76	387	294	79	106	33	77	1397	184	404	100	666	20	18	17	112	39	108	46	61	29	32	199	166	35	4	3.71	.48	1.07	.27	1.78	.06	.05	.05	.29	.11	.27	.12	.15	.07	.09	.50	.43	.09	.01
11	59.94	592	431	121	166	50	94	2573	277	767	143	1285	79	52	34	214	68	176	69	106	49	40	278	279	32	8	4.42	.47	1.31	.25	2.22	.14	.09	.06	.37	.11	.30	.12	.18	.08	.07	.49	.47	.06	.02
12	58.55	512	373	95	141	43	94	2195	235	627	147	1115	65	32	20	145	93	141	70	71	48	36	242	252	31	12	4.25	.45	1.22	.28	2.15	.12	.06	.04	.28	.18	.27	.14	.14	.09	.07	.47	.49	.06	.02
13	57.93	419	383	108	141	48	87	1956	262	553	128	957	50	30	28	151	74	90	33	57	36	32	205	187	32	7	4.74	.62	1.34	.32	2.33	.12	.07	.07	.36	.18	.22	.08	.14	.09	.08	.50	.45	.07	.02
14	48.10	489	467	128	178	58	104	2671	317	744	165	1375	95	58	30	158	45	192	79	112	55	26	233	243	28	3	5.49	.64	1.53	.34	2.83	.19	.11	.06	.32	.09	.40	.16	.23	.12	.06	.49	.50	.06	.01
15	48.10	54	56	9	22	4	21	143	13	44	7	75	5	2	2	11	11	5	3	2	1	5	13	14	1	2	5.07	.48	1.83	.23	2.59	.19	.09	.09	.41	.28	.17	.11	.05	.01	.19	.41	.44	.02	.06
16	48.10	233	249	56	96	26	71	1025	111	318	56	515	29	15	12	80	37	63	26	37	14	25	127	88	9	3	4.44	.48	1.39	.24	2.23	.12	.06	.05	.34	.16	.26	.11	.15	.06	.12	.55	.38	.03	.02
17	46.40	810	480	130	184	61	104	3618	399	1068	188	1791	145	43	47	233	191	220	125	95	28	30	290	503	28	11	4.46	.49	1.32	.24	2.22	.18	.05	.06	.28	.24	.27	.15	.12	.03	.04	.35	.62	.03	.01
18	46.40	223	198	40	77	22	59	828	84	259	43	407	21	11	11	59	54	48	18	29	11	25	86	104	8	6	4.05	.41	1.27	.20	1.99	.10	.05	.06	.24	.21	.23	.08	.15	.06	.13	.42	.51	.04	.03
19	46.40	377	332	96	121	32	84	1677	206	499	76	832	45	24	23	128	68	99	42	56	32	33	200	154	20	4	4.40	.54	1.32	.20	2.19	.12	.06	.06	.33	.18	.26	.11	.15	.09	.09	.52	.41	.05	.01
20	36.84	193	215	44	83	22	65	808	76	259	42	399	19	12	9	57	34	59	26	34	23	38	62	99	6	5	4.36	.41	1.40	.23	2.14	.12	.07	.05	.30	.18	.31	.14	.17	.12	.20	.34	.51	.03	.03
21	36.38	177	249	56	95	27	70	930	103	272	55	471	31	17	9	66	28	50	23	27	14	20	64	99	6	5	5.39	.58	1.58	.33	2.70	.17	.10	.05	.35	.15	.31	.15	.16	.09	.16	.35	.56	.03	.03
22	34.73	357	307	77	114	36	80	1468	171	451	79	713	47	24	18	112	67	112	49	64	32	31	162	157	19	4	4.36	.50	1.35	.24	2.11	.14	.07	.06	.27	.19	.33	.14	.19	.10	.09	.49	.48	.06	.01

23	31.90	221	212	51	78	19	64	830	100	233	37	408	21	8	7	47	62	45	22	23	6	36	70	114	4	6	2	3.94	.47	1.09	.10	.04	.03	.22	.31	.21	.11	.10	.03	.20	.34	.54	.01	.03
24	30.18	165	109	26	39	7	38	443	58	118	13	222	7	5	4	27	34	29	15	14	2	22	67	65	10	12	6	3.10	.36	.85	.06	.03	.02	.14	.21	.20	.09	.11	.02	.20	.37	.43	.05	.02
25	29.33	216	219	45	84	27	63	828	84	247	56	408	23	16	7	67	42	42	22	20	8	21	107	95	12	12	6	3.67	.35	1.11	.09	.06	.03	.29	.19	.21	.11	.10	.04	.12	.49	.44	.05	.03
26	27.09	451	283	70	110	29	74	1697	195	528	69	870	36	21	25	135	96	110	45	65	24	52	152	268	19	19	12	3.82	.43	1.20	.08	.05	.03	.30	.24	.24	.11	.14	.05	.13	.32	.59	.04	.03
27	23.58	141	150	28	59	12	51	526	54	164	20	264	14	7	9	35	39	32	15	17	4	18	85	60	4	4	5	3.82	.38	1.16	.11	.04	.06	.26	.22	.22	.13	.11	.03	.17	.44	.43	.03	.04
28	23.07	356	206	40	87	16	63	1221	132	390	44	567	23	11	21	81	110	85	39	47	5	48	124	194	6	6	16	3.45	.37	1.10	.07	.03	.06	.22	.30	.24	.10	.13	.01	.15	.36	.55	.02	.04
29	23.06	378	360	100	131	41	88	1912	219	554	121	914	59	26	26	134	57	101	39	62	36	40	173	177	16	6	7	5.09	.58	1.47	.16	.07	.07	.36	.15	.27	.16	.16	.09	.11	.45	.47	.04	.02
30	21.89	270	197	42	77	20	57	805	99	226	40	417	18	10	8	49	52	50	31	19	5	22	105	114	6	7	7	3.43	.42	.96	.08	.03	.03	.21	.21	.21	.10	.08	.02	.10	.46	.49	.03	.03
31	20.86	511	380	105	140	42	92	2353	280	700	107	1124	72	35	19	146	91	189	83	104	60	33	237	253	26	11	11	4.68	.55	1.39	.14	.04	.04	.29	.17	.37	.13	.20	.12	.07	.47	.49	.05	.02
32	19.97	321	191	37	74	16	64	948	93	285	34	497	14	14	13	66	78	79	44	34	8	34	177	122	12	12	5	2.94	.28	.88	.10	.07	.04	.20	.25	.24	.16	.10	.02	.12	.55	.38	.03	.04
33	18.12	82	108	17	39	8	44	268	27	76	12	142	6	3	2	17	21	21	15	6	1	15	47	24	3	3	11	3.24	.32	.92	.08	.05	.05	.21	.26	.26	.18	.08	.01	.20	.56	.29	.03	.06
34	18.12	226	214	44	82	21	66	826	80	244	42	415	15	9	10	63	52	56	33	23	9	28	127	77	16	16	11	3.68	.36	1.09	.10	.04	.05	.28	.23	.23	.15	.10	.04	.13	.56	.34	.07	.05
35	17.88	255	210	50	80	16	64	862	102	257	32	439	21	11	12	50	40	90	36	54	9	32	108	122	12	12	2	3.38	.39	1.01	.12	.05	.07	.19	.16	.25	.14	.21	.03	.13	.41	.48	.04	.01
36	17.63	426	304	105	147	45	88	2088	231	640	115	1036	69	30	30	162	83	112	45	67	38	39	172	221	10	10	12	4.81	.53	1.48	.16	.07	.07	.37	.35	.35	.16	.16	.09	.10	.40	.52	.02	.03
37	10.00	248	187	42	71	18	55	752	85	241	33	379	17	7	8	48	73	40	18	22	5	23	108	86	11	11	7	3.54	.38	1.15	.08	.03	.04	.22	.27	.22	.11	.11	.10	.11	.49	.42	.05	.03
38	10.00	64	91	14	36	6	36	231	22	71	9	118	5	3	2	16	17	15	8	7	1	11	30	21	1	1	4	3.83	.34	1.15	.10	.05	.03	.24	.28	.24	.15	.13	.11	.21	.45	.35	.02	.06
39	10.00	104	119	21	46	9	43	400	43	121	17	203	13	4	5	26	41	20	11	9	2	24	47	39	3	3	5	3.95	.40	1.19	.13	.04	.04	.23	.19	.25	.12	.07	.12	.21	.44	.37	.03	.05
40	10.00	191	161	31	62	15	52	606	62	191	31	302	13	6	5	36	33	33	19	14	3	31	93	73	6	6	10	3.41	.33	1.06	.08	.03	.03	.19	.40	.19	.10	.10	.07	.28	.47	.40	.01	.07
41	10.00	217	175	26	76	14	59	761	66	251	25	394	20	12	8	47	92	35	21	13	3	37	121	63	6	6	32	3.51	.30	1.16	.09	.05	.04	.21	.44	.21	.06	.06	.10	.22	.54	.29	.02	.15
42	10.00	241	201	40	84	18	59	947	96	298	41	484	28	14	12	73	77	37	21	15	5	35	82	108	5	5	5	4.35	.43	1.39	.15	.07	.05	.32	.37	.32	.09	.06	.02	.19	.37	.49	.02	.08
Average family		341	277	70	105	30	72	1440	165	423	78	719	41	22	17	105	62	90	40	49	23	30	151	163	17	17	7	4.17	.46	1.24	.12	.06	.05	.29	.21	.26	.12	.14	.06	.12	.45	.45	.04	.03
r with SES		.57	.65	.68	.62	.67	.61	.60	.62	.57	.68	.61	.51	.65	.48	.65	ns	ns	.57	*	.59	ns	.59	.54		.74	*	*	.57	ns	.61	*	ns	.54	*	.63	ns	.53	-.62	ns	*	.65	-.63
Interrater agreement		.95	1.00	1.00	1.00	1.00	1.00	.97	1.00	1.00	1.00	.84	.84	.84	.84	.84	.84	.84	.84	.84	.84	ns	.99	.99	.99	.74	.84	.97																
Split-half reliability		.97	.97	.96	.96	.89	.98	.97	.97	.97	.99	.99	.92	.97	.97	.95	.98	.96	.90	.97	.85	.53	.97	.97	.95	.92	.96	.93	.95	.96	.96	.97	.88	.92	.97	.92	.93	.94						
Partial r = Utterances		.91	.92	.95	.89	.99	.99	.96	.99	.99	.96	.94	.95	.94	.98	.98	.94	.85	.97	.97	.92	.66	.72	.91																			
Richness		.09	.79	.63	.91	.48	.80	.88	.88	.91	.87	.88	.68	.83	.89	.86	.87	.90	.86	.83	.72	.89																				
r with Vocabulary Growth	*	.62	.62	.58	.65	.63	.49	.47	*	.52	.59	.57	.49	.59	.57	.48	.52	.52	*	*	.63	*	.68	.50	*	.60	.56	-.59	.47	-.67	.66	-.56										
Vocabulary Use	.54	.72	.71	.70	.75	.72	.62	.59	*	.60	.69	.62	.61	.58	.57	*	.58	.58	*	*	.68	*	.69	.57	*	.69	.60	-.56	.51	-.65	.61	-.69										
Stanford-Binet IQ	ns	.51	.53	.48	.53	.52	*	.50	*	.49	.54	*	.54	*	.49	ns	.53	.60	*	ns	.55	ns	.66	.53	ns	.63	.47	-.54		-.69	.53	-.57										

Note: Numbers, $p < .001$; *, $p\ .001 < .01$; ns, $p > .01$.

Appendix B
Figures

◆ ◆ ◆ ◆

The spontaneous speech data we recorded in our preschool research during the War on Poverty showed that the rate at which the Turner House children were adding words to the vocabulary in daily use was markedly slower than the rate at which the professors' children were adding words. Projecting the developmental trajectories of the vocabulary growth curves we could see an ever-widening gap between the vocabulary resources the children would bring to reading in school. When we saw that our interventions at age 4 could not close the gap we realized we needed to find out what was happening in children's early experience that could be influencing these developmental trajectories.

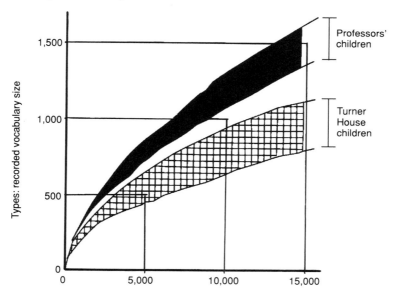

Figure 1. Range in the cumulative type/token curves constructed from a year of daily, identically recorded 15-minute samples of spontaneous speech during preschool free play for 12 professors' children (solid curve) and for 11 Turner House children (hatched curve) from a poverty neighborhood. The type/token curves of the professors' children all fell within the black area. The curves for the Turner House children all fell within the hatched area. (Adapted from Hart & Risley, 1981.)

233

When we analyzed the data from 2½ years of observing for 1 hour each month the unstructured interactions at home between children and parents in 42 families of varying size, socioeconomic status, and ethnic background, we saw differences in rates of vocabulary growth among the children similar to those we had seen in our preschool research. By age 3 some children were as far above the average in vocabulary resources as other children were below; we saw a widening gap beginning as early as age 24 months. But now we could examine the observational data for differences in the children's early experience.

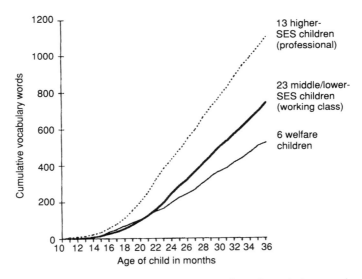

Figure 2.   At each month the average number of vocabulary words recorded in that and all prior months for three groups of children from the time the children were 10 months old until they were 36 months old. The children were grouped by the socioeconomic index assigned to the occupation of their parents (see Chapter 4, endnote 3). The 13 higher-SES children (dotted line) were in professional families, 23 middle-lower SES children (heavy solid line) were in working-class families, and 6 welfare children (light solid line) were in families receiving welfare (Aid to Families with Dependent Children).

Over the 2 years of observation every family varied from month to month in the amount of talking and interacting the parents did with their children. We asked parents to just "do what you usually do" at home with the child, and we designed the study to collect an amount of data that would allow us to use averages to reveal the stable patterns within the continual variability that characterizes the everyday parenting of a developing child. The most stable difference between families was in the amount of talking that went on: Parents who differed in amount of talking stayed different even as they varied from month to month.

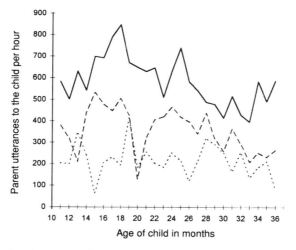

Figure 3. Average number of utterances addressed to the child per hour each month by the parent in three different families: a professional (solid line), a working-class (dashed line), and a welfare (dotted line) family by SES. The families were selected to illustrate in one figure the month-to-month variability seen in individual families representative of the SES groups in terms of both amount of talking and overall trends across time. The families are those with Rank 11, 22, and 41 in Appendix A.

The most striking difference between families was in how much interaction and talking typically went on in the home. Some families spent up to four times as much time interacting with their children as did others; some parents said much more than other parents to 1- and 2-year old children per hour of daily life. When we examined family factors, we saw that the time and amount of talking that went on in the family did not vary systematically with the gender of the child, the ethnic background of the family, the birth of a new baby, or if both parents were working. But time and talk *were* associated with the socioeconomic status of the family: Parents in professional families characteristically devoted over half again more time and said three times as much to their children as did parents in welfare families.

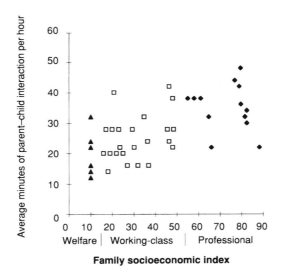

Family socioeconomic index

Figure 4. Average number of minutes per hour that each of the 42 parents spent in interactions with the child. Number of minutes was averaged for six observations: when the children were 16–17 months old, 24–25 months old, and 32–33 months old (see Chapter 3, endnote 6). The horizontal axis = SEI, or the socioeconomic index number assigned to parent occupation (see Chapter 3, endnote 4); the labels summarize into SES groups the occupations in the index. The vertical axis = average minutes per hour interacting. Minutes interacting includes all talk between child and parent, that is, time when either the child or the parent was actually speaking to the other.

236

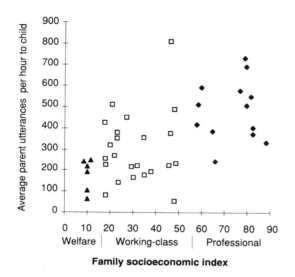

Figure 5.   Average number of utterances per hour that each of the 42 parents addressed to the child. Utterances were averaged for all 24 observation hours when the children were 13–36 months old (see Appendix A and Chapter 6, endnote 3). The horizontal axis = SEI (see Chapter 3, endnote 4; and Appendix A); the labels summarize into SES groups the occupations in the index (within the working-class group, scores are below 31 for blue-collar occupations and above 31 for white-collar occupations). Note how different was the amount of talk at the extremes in advantage and the marked variety in amount of talk within the working-class families.

The differences we saw between families in the amount of talking and interaction were so substantial that we checked both how consistent individual families were over time and how characteristic the differences were of population groups with the relative advantages summarized in SES. Statistical tests, reliability assessments, and verification in split halves of the data (see Chapter 6, endnotes 3 and 5) showed us that the families were astonishingly consistent in relative sociability and that the SES groups were characteristically different in average amounts of talking and time spent interacting with 1- and 2-year-old children.

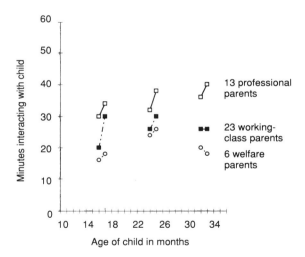

Figure 6. Average number of minutes per hour parents in three SES groups spent interacting with their children in six sample observations. The data are the same as those shown in Figure 4, but in Figure 4 the data from the six samples were averaged by individual parent; here the same data are averaged for each month by SES group. The vertical axis = average minutes per hour interacting. Minutes interacting includes all time when either the child or the parent was actually speaking to the other. Shown are data averaged for 13 professional parents (open squares), 23 working-class parents (solid squares), and 6 welfare parents (open circles).

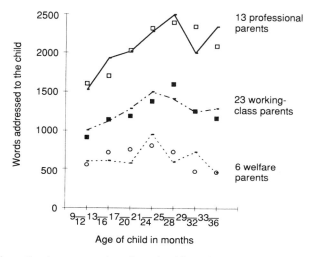

Figure 7. Average number of words addressed to the child by parents in three SES groups with the database split into halves. The horizontal axis = age of the child in months; the vertical axis = words to the child per hour. Lines connect even-numbered months; squares and circles mark odd-numbered months. Each point shows the average of 2 months; for example, the first dot on the line is the average of the two observations recorded for the even-numbered data months when the children were 10 and 12 months old. The squares and circle at the same point are the average of the two observations recorded for the odd-numbered data months when the children were 9 and 11 months old. Data are averaged for 13 professional parents (solid line, open squares), 23 working-class parents (dashed line, solid squares), and 6 welfare parents (dotted line, open circles).

After we defined and quantified the quality features of parent language and interaction, analyses showed that by the time children were 3 years old, families differing in SES had provided their children vastly different amounts of experience with language used to convey information and affect. Lots of talking did not dilute the richness of quality features in the utterances the children heard but served to increase the amount of experience children had with nearly all the quality features of language and interaction.

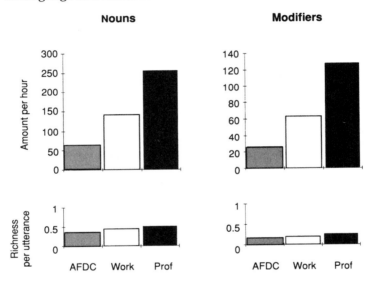

Nouns **Modifiers**

Figure 8.   Average number per hour (amount, top graphs) and per utterance (richness, bottom graphs) of nouns (left graphs) and modifiers (adjectives and adverbs, right graphs) the parents in three SES groups addressed to children 13–36 months of age. (Note the different scales on the graphs.) Six parents (AFDC, shaded bars) were on welfare, 23 parents (Work, open bars) were working class, and 13 parents (Prof, solid bars) were professionals. (The data are averaged from Appendix A.) Across SES families were somewhat different in the richness of vocabulary in the utterances they addressed to their children, but the large differences in the amount of that speech resulted in even larger differences in the amount of experience with these quality features they provided their children in the 2 years the children were learning to talk.

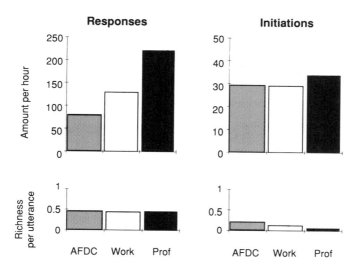

Figure 9. Average number per hour (amount, top graphs) and per utterance (richness, bottom graphs) of responses (left graphs) and initiations (right graphs) the parents in three SES groups addressed to children 13–36 months of age. (Note the different scales on the graphs.) Responses were utterances immediately contingent on a child's vocal, verbal, or nonverbal behavior; initiations were utterances addressed to the child after 5 seconds or more of no interaction. Six parents (AFDC, shaded bars) were on welfare, 23 parents (Work, open bars) were working class, and 13 parents (Prof, solid bars) were professionals. (The data are averaged from Appendix A.) Across SES children's experience differed greatly in the amount of responses per hour they received from their parents, which remained proportional to the amount of parent talk. However, differences in amount of parent talk were not related to how often parents initiated interaction with their children, which remained constant across SES groups.

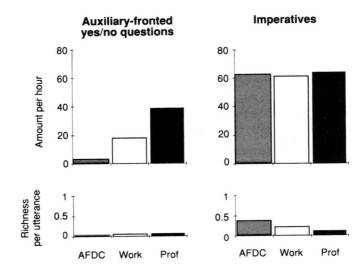

Figure 10.   Average number per hour (amount, top graphs) and per utterance (richness, bottom graphs) of auxiliary-fronted yes/no questions (left graphs) and imperatives (right graphs) the parents in three SES groups addressed to children 13–36 months old. Imperatives directed children to comply ("Do as I say"); auxiliary-fronted yes/no questions asked for compliance ("Can you do that?"). Six parents (AFDC, shaded bars) were on welfare, 23 parents (Work, open bars) were working class, and 13 parents (Prof, solid bars) were professionals. (The data are averaged from Appendix A.) Across SES children's experience differed in both the amount and richness of auxiliary-fronted yes/no questions they heard but not in the number of directives they were given. Lesser amounts of welfare parents' talk, however, served to make imperatives a more prominent part of their children's experience.

Differences in the amount of parent talk contributed more to the amount of children's experience with the quality features of language and interaction than did differences in the richness of these features in parent utterances. Because the relative richness of the quality features in parent utterances varied so little, all the children had more experience with the quality features of language and interaction when their parents talked more.

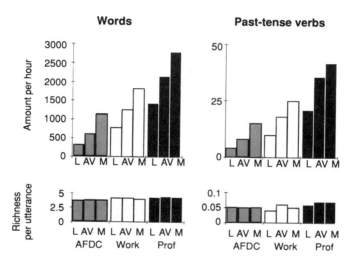

Words   **Past-tense verbs**

Figure 11. Average number per hour (amount, top graphs) and per utterance (richness, bottom graphs) of the words (left graphs) and past-tense verbs (right graphs) parents in three SES groups addressed to their children in an average hour (AV), in the 3 hours they talked least (L), and in the 3 hours they talked most (M), to their children. (Note the different scales on the graphs.) The number of words and past-tense verbs in an average hour (AV) was averaged over the months the children were 13–36 months old (see Appendix A). The averages in the 3 hours the parents talked least (L) and most (M) are from observations when the children were at the beginning (11–19 months old), middle (20–28 months old), and end (29–36 months old) of the process of learning to talk (see Chapter 6, endnote 7). Of the parents, 13 (Prof, solid bars) were professionals, 23 (Work, open bars) were working class, and 6 (AFDC, shaded bars) were on welfare.

For each SES group there was a similar spread between the periods of least and most talk; the absolute differences between the groups remained unchanged. The richness of words in parent utterances and of past-tense verb forms varied little; all the children had proportionately more experience hearing words of all kinds and talking about past events when their parents talked more to them.

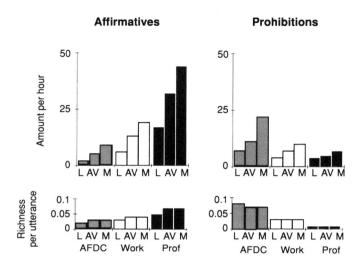

Figure 12. Average number per hour (amount, top graphs) and per utterance (richness, bottom graphs) of affirmatives (left graphs) and prohibitions (right graphs) parents in three SES groups addressed to their children in an average hour (AV), in the 3 hours they talked least (L), and in the 3 hours they talked most (M) to their children. The number in an average hour (AV) was averaged over the months the children were 13–36 months old (see Appendix A). The averages in the 3 hours the parents talked least (L) and most (M) are from observations early, middle, and late in the period that the children were learning to talk (see Chapter 6, endnote 7). Of the parents, 13 (Prof, solid bars) were professionals, 23 (Work, open bars) were working class, and 6 (AFDC, shaded bars) were on welfare.

Affirmatives were parent encouragements that explicitly approved the child's behavior or repeated or rephrased what the child said; prohibitions were parent discouragements that explicitly disapproved or prohibited the child's behavior (see Chapter 6, endnote 4). All the children heard more feedback, both encouraging and discouraging, when their parents talked to them more.

From the quality features of language and interaction we quantified in the data, we chose logical combinations of features that would exemplify the categories of significant family experience we saw provided to children in everyday parenting (see Chapter 7, Table 2, and the figures on the pages that follow). Children had differing amounts of experience with the Language Diversity contributed by lots of talk; with the relative encouragement and discouragement contained in Feedback Tone; with Symbolic Emphasis on names, relations, and recall; with a Guidance Style focused on asking rather than demanding; and with the Responsiveness that focused on the child's contributions to interactions. Experience with these five categories of significant family experience adds to breadth of knowledge, analytic and symbolic competencies, self-confidence, and problem solving, which are among the interlocking attitudes, skills, and knowledge children bring to school and work.

The amount of experience that children had in the first 3 years with these categories of significant family experience was strongly predictive of the children's accomplishments at age 3 and at age 9–10. For each category of significant family experience, the strong relationship with SES is apparent: at the extremes in advantage the children in professional families are seen to receive high amounts of experience and the children in the welfare families low amounts of experience. Between the extremes the marked variety within the American working class is notable: Some working-class children received high amounts of experience and others low amounts, and there is no relationship between the socioeconomic status of the family and amount of experience.

Language Diversity

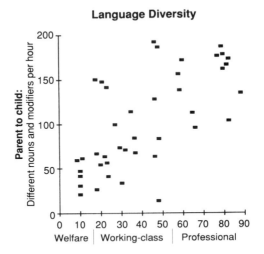

Family socioeconomic index

Figure 13. Parent Language Diversity averaged for each of the 42 parents over all 24 observation hours when the children were 13–36 months old (see Chapter 7, Table 3). Language Diversity denotes the amount of a child's experience with language, as exemplified by the sum of different nouns, adjectives, and adverbs addressed to the child per hour. Family socioeconomic index is the SEI number assigned to parent occupation (see Chapter 3, endnote 4, and Appendix A). The labels are those used to group occupations in the index. By age 3 some children had had much more experience than others in hearing different objects, actions, attributes, relations, and conceptual categories named and described. The amount of children's experience with Language Diversity was strongly associated with the magnitude of their accomplishments at age 3 and at age 9–10 (see Table 3). Note how different was the amount of children's experience at the extremes in advantage and the marked variety of children's experience within the working-class families.

Appendix B

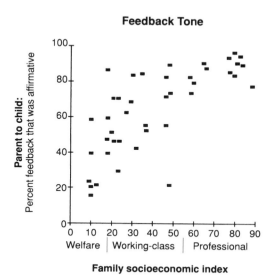

Feedback Tone

Figure 14.   Parent Feedback Tone averaged for each of the 42 parents over all 24 observation hours when the children were 13–36 months old (see Table 3). Feedback Tone denotes the prevailing affect of parent–child interactions, as exemplified by the ratio of affirmative feedback (parent repetitions, expansions, extensions of child utterances, plus explicit approval of children's words and actions with words such as "good" and "right") to total feedback (affirmatives plus prohibitions directing "Don't," "Stop," "Quit," "Shut up" and explicit disapproval with words such as "bad" and "wrong"). Family socioeconomic index is the SEI number assigned to parent occupation (see Chapter 3, endnote 4, and Appendix A). Some children had much more experience than others with the parent encouragement that contributes to self-esteem, confidence, and motivation. The amount of children's experience with encouraging feedback was strongly associated with the magnitude of their accomplishments at age 3 and at age 9–10 (see Table 3). Note how different was the amount of children's experience with affirmative feedback at the extremes in advantage and the marked variety of children's experience within the working-class families.

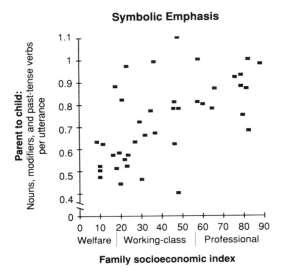

Symbolic Emphasis

Family socioeconomic index

Figure 15. Parent Symbolic Emphasis averaged for each of the 42 parents over all 24 observation hours when the children were 13–36 months old (see Table 3). Symbolic Emphasis denotes the symbolic richness of a child's social experience as exemplified in the number of nouns, adjectives, adverbs, and past-tense verbs a child heard per parent utterance. Family socioeconomic index is the SEI number assigned to parent occupation (see Chapter 3, endnote 4). Hearing words as symbols used for naming, recalling, and relating information was a consistent attribute of some children's interactions with their parents. Symbolic Emphasis was strongly associated with the magnitude of their accomplishments at age 3 and age 9–10 (see Table 3). Again, note how different was the children's experience with Symbolic Emphasis at the extremes in advantage and the marked variety of children's experience within the working-class families.

Family socioeconomic index

Figure 16.   Parent Guidance Style averaged for each of the 42 parents over all 24 observation hours when the children were 13–36 months old (see Table 3). Guidance Style denotes the amount of children's experience with opportunities to choose as exemplified by the ratio of auxiliary-fronted yes/no questions ("Can you. . ." "Do you. . .") to all directives (auxiliary-fronted yes/no questions plus imperatives). Family socioeconomic index is the SEI number assigned to parent occupation (see Chapter 3, endnote 4, and Appendix A). Some children had much more experience than others with being asked rather than told to behave in more mature ways. The amount of children's experience with polite guidance that offered choices was strongly associated with the magnitude of their accomplishments at age 3 and age 9–10 (see Table 3). Note how different was the children's experience with polite guidance at the extremes in advantage and the marked variety of children's experience within the working-class families.

Responsiveness

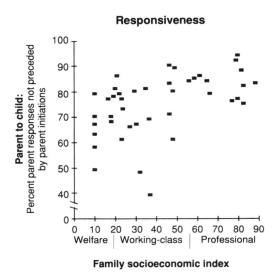

Family socioeconomic index

Figure 17. Parent Responsiveness averaged for each of the 42 parents across all 24 observation hours when the children were 13–36 months old (see Table 3). Responsiveness denotes the relative importance of the child's behavior during family interactions as exemplified by the ratio of noninitiating parent responses (parent responses minus parent initiations) to all parent responses. Family socioeconomic index is the SEI number assigned to parent occupation (see Chapter 3, endnote 4, and Appendix A). Some children had more experience than others with parent responsiveness that focused on appreciating the words and topics the children contributed to interactions. The children's experience with responsiveness was strongly associated with the magnitude of their accomplishments at age 3 (see Table 3).

We had undertaken the longitudinal study to find out what was happening in children's early experience. We disassembled the interactions we observed into molecular components we could reliably code and count. We examined the correlations between the quantities of each of those components and measures of the children's language competence. Based on those correlations, our understanding of the literature, and the impressions of patterns of parenting we had absorbed during thousands of hours of observing, we reassembled the quantities into five derived variables (see Chapter 7, Table 3, and Figures 13–17). We entered all five derived variables into multiple regression analyses with the measures of the children's accomplishments.

We found that the five derived variables together not only uniformly marked the SES extremes of the families we observed but also robustly predicted the accomplishments of the working-class children. Together they accounted for 60% of the variance in the children's accomplishments at age 3 (see Chapter 7, Table 4). We conclude that these variables are not simply marker variables denoting social class or subculture but powerful aspects of parenting that cause important outcomes in children.

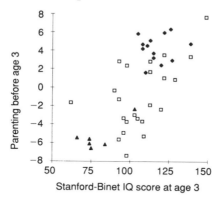

Figure 18. For each of the 42 children, the parenting provided the child before age 3 plotted against the child's Stanford-Binet IQ score at age 3. Parenting is the sum of the z-scores for the five derived variables (Language Diversity, Feedback Tone, Symbolic Emphasis, Guidance Style, Responsiveness; see Table 3). Shown are individual data for 13 professional families (diamonds), 23 working-class families (open squares), and 6 welfare families (triangles). Parenting not only strongly predicted IQ scores at the extremes in advantage but predicted equally strongly the IQ scores of the 23 working-class children (see Table 4).

Our more than 2 years of regular observations in family homes, carefully checked and analyzed, showed the consistency of the amount of the categories of significant family experience parents were providing their children. We extrapolated the relative differences we saw in the longitudinal data in order to estimate children's cumulative experience in the first 4 years of life and so glimpse the magnitude of the problem facing an intervention planned to equalize the early experience of welfare and working-class children. Even if we have overestimated by half the differences between children in amounts of cumulative experience the gap is so great by age 4 that the best that can be expected from education or intervention is to keep children from falling still farther behind. For an intervention to keep an average welfare child's experience equal in amount to that of an average working-class child would require that the child be in substitute care comparable to the average in a professional home for 40 hours per week from birth onward.

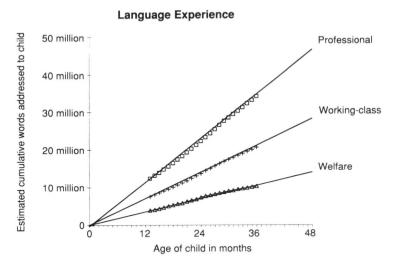

Language Experience

Figure 19. Cumulative number of words addressed to the child in 13 professional (squares), 23 working-class (plus signs), and 6 welfare families (triangles) extrapolated from birth to 12 months of age and from 37 to 48 months of child age. The linear regression line was fit to the actual average cumulative number of words addressed to the children per hour when they were 12–36 months old.

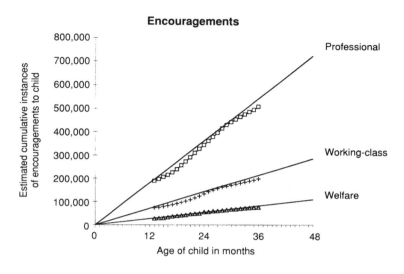

Encouragements

Discouragements

Figure 20. Cumulative instances of feedback containing encouragements (top graph) and discouragements (bottom graph) addressed to the child in 13 professional (squares), 23 working-class (plus signs), and 6 welfare (triangles) families extrapolated from birth to 12 months of age and from 37 to 48 months of child age. Encouragements were affirmations that repeated, extended, or expanded the child's utterances and expressions of approval of the child's behavior as "right" or "good." Discouragements were prohibitions directing the child "Don't," "Stop," "Quit," or "Shut up" and expressions of disapproval of the child's behavior as "bad" or "wrong." Note the reversal of the lines in the bottom graph, reflecting the prevailing negative Feedback Tone in the welfare homes. The linear regression lines were fit to the actual average cumulative numbers of affirmations and prohibitions addressed to the children per hour when they were 12–36 months old.

Index

Page numbers followed by "f" indicate figures; numbers followed by "t" indicate tables; numbers followed by "n" indicate notes.

changing trends in, 203, 217n
coding, 63, 73n
of parents in longitudinal study,
30–31, 62–63
social distinctions based on, 203
and socioeconomic status, 63
see also Socioeconomic status

Parent(s)
helping, alternatives for, 212–214,
219n
in longitudinal study
availability of both, and amount
of parental talk to child, 62
everyday talk of, 130–131
interactions with child(ren), *see*
Parent–child interactions
language, *see* Language, parental
occupation, *see* Occupation
similarities among, 53–56
vocabulary pretest for, 176, 189n
Parent–child interactions
and children's language experience,
21–22, 50n, 54–55, 75–76,
91–92, 97, 102, 112–114,
115n–117n
quality features of, 76, 102–111
see also Adjacency conditions;
Discourse function; Quality
features; Valence
social implications of, 113, 115n,
116n, 117n
verbatim examples of, 77–90
Parenting, 22, 49n, 75–76
difficulties of, in modern America,
210–212
in longitudinal study, everyday
challenges of, xii, 55–57
characteristics of, 75–93
child accomplishment and, 158,
159f, 165–168, 168t, 251f
definition of, 168t
styles, 91–92, 102–103
children's learning about,
102–103
in working-class families, diversity of, 179

Peabody Picture Vocabulary
Test–Revised, 160–161,
171n–173n
scores at age 9–10
child accomplishments at age 3
and, 156t–157t, 160–161
early family experience and,
156t–157t, 161–162
relation to family socioeconomic
status and parenting, 161–162,
167–168, 168t
Poverty
children's language acquisition
and, x, xii
culture of poverty, 1–2, 15–16, 18n,
204
see also Socioeconomic status;
Turner House children;
Welfare families
PPVT–R *see* Peabody Picture Vocabulary Test–Revised
Professional families
advantages of children in, and
emerging subculture in American society, 204
characteristics of, 32t, 69
child's cumulative experience of
affirmatives and prohibitions
in, 198–200, 200f, 253
child's cumulative language experience in, 197–198, 198f, 252
child's early experience with language in
amount and richness of,
123–130, 123f–125f, 128f,
217n, 240–242, 243–244
extrapolating amounts of,
131–133, 197–200, 198f, 200f,
252, 253f
and number of words heard in
first 3 years of life, 132–133,
197–198
and number of words heard per
hour, 132, 197
child's language acquisition in, x
child's language use in, 9–10
parent–child similarities in, 176t,
177

Symbolic Emphasis, 149*t*, 152, 152*f*,
156*t*–157*t*, 170*n*–172*n*, 192,
245, 248*f*
and child accomplishments at age
3, 155–158, 248, 251
definition of, 149*t*, 152, 171*n*
and family socioeconomic status,
152*f*, 165–166, 168*t*, 248
and test performance in third
grade, 156*t*–157*t*, 161–162,
167–168
in working-class families, related
to child accomplishments,
166–168, 248*f*

Talking, *see* Parent–child interactions; Utterances
Television
children's learning from, 101, 116*n*
and cultural diversity, 58
use of, in families observed
amount of, 39, 74*n*
variability in, 69, 70
Test of Language Development–2:
Intermediate, 160–161,
170*n*–173*n*
scores at age 9–10
child accomplishments at age 3
and, 156*t*–157*t*, 160–161
early family experience and,
156*t*–157*t*, 161–162
relation to family socioeconomic
status and parenting, 161–162,
167–168, 168*t*
Test performance, in third grade
child accomplishments at age 3
and, 156*t*–157*t*, 160–161
family experience and, 161–162
measurement, 160–161, 170*n*–173*n*
reading comprehension scores
at age 9–10, child accom-
plishments at age 3 and,
160–161
relation to family socioeconomic
status and parenting, 161–162,
167–168, 168*t*
Time spent interacting with children,
64–66, 65*f*, 68*f*, 74*n*, 236*f*, 238*f*

TOLD, *see* Test of Language Development–2: Intermediate
Turner House Preschool
children in
demographics, 9, 163
vocabulary resources of, 10
children's language use in, comparison with professors' children,
9–10
children's vocabulary growth in
comparison with professors'
children, 10–12, 11*f*, 162–165,
233*f*
hypotheses about, 12–15
intervention for, 12–15
intervention at, 4–6
assumptions underlying, 8
design of effective teaching
strategies, 7–8, 18*n*–19*n*, 117*n*
on spontaneous speech, 7–8
on vocabulary growth rate,
12–15

Utterances
amount and richness compared,
126–130
coding, for database construction,
44–46
reliability of, 136*n*, 228–229
definition of, 138*n*
parental, to children, 145
as rephrasing or verbatim repetition, analysis of, 135*n*
variability by socioeconomic status, 59–61, 60*f*, 61–63, 65*f*,
123–126, 235*f*, 237*f*
parent–child similarities, 176, 176*t*

Valence, 102–103, 109–111, 149*t*
coding, for database construction,
44, 96–97
coding in data variables, 111
Verbs, 43, 95–99
amount and richness averaged at
13–36 months, 228–229
child accomplishments and, 146

265